The
CORE SIX

The CORE SIX

Essential Strategies

for Achieving Excellence

with the Common Core

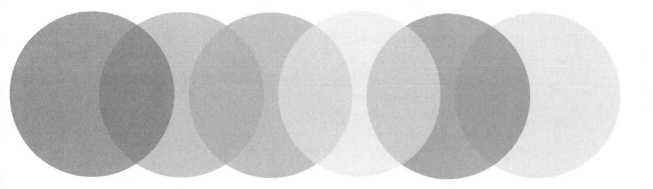

Harvey F. Silver | R. Thomas Dewing | Matthew J. Perini

Foreword by Heidi Hayes Jacobs

 Alexandria, VA USA

ASCD®

1703 N. Beauregard St. • Alexandria, VA 22311-1714 USA
Phone: 800-933-2723 or 703-578-9600 • Fax: 703-575-5400
Website: www.ascd.org • E-mail: member@ascd.org
Author guidelines: www.ascd.org/write

Gene R. Carter, *Executive Director;* Ed Milliken, *Interim Chief Program Development Officer;* Carole Hayward, *Interim Publisher;* Genny Ostertag, *Acquisitions Editor;* Julie Houtz, *Director, Book Editing & Production;* Miriam Goldstein, *Editor;* Louise Bova, *Senior Graphic Designer;* Mike Kalyan, *Production Manager;* Valerie Younkin, *Desktop Publishing Specialist;* Kyle Steichen, *Production Specialist*

Printed in the United States of America. Cover art © 2012 by ASCD. ASCD publications present a variety of viewpoints. The views expressed or implied in this book should not be interpreted as official positions of the Association.

All web links in this book are correct as of the publication date below but may have become inactive or otherwise modified since that time. If you notice a deactivated or changed link, please e-mail books@ascd.org with the words "Link Update" in the subject line. In your message, please specify the web link, the book title, and the page number on which the link appears.

PAPERBACK ISBN: 978-1-4166-1475-3   ASCD product #113007   n8/12

Also available as an e-book (see Books in Print for the ISBNs).

Quantity discounts: 10–49 copies, 10%; 50+ copies, 15%; for 1,000 or more copies, call 800-933-2723, ext. 5634, or 703-575-5634. For desk copies: www.ascd.org/deskcopy

Library of Congress Cataloging-in-Publication Data
Silver, Harvey F.
  The core six : essential strategies for achieving excellence with the common core / Harvey F. Silver, R. Thomas Dewing, and Matthew J. Perini ; foreword by Heidi Hayes Jacobs.
    p. cm.
  Includes bibliographical references and index.
  ISBN 978-1-4166-1475-3 (pbk. : alk. paper)
  1. Education—Curricula—Standards—United States. I. Dewing, R. Thomas. II. Perini, Matthew J., 1973– III. Title.
  LB3060.83.S576 2012
  375'.001—dc23
                                                              2012021294

22 21 20 19 18 17 16 15 14 13 12   2 3 4 5 6 7 8 9 10 11 12

The Core Six: Essential Strategies for Achieving Excellence with the Common Core

Foreword

Heidi Hayes Jacobs

The word *core* has special meaning for educators. *Core* suggests what is essential, what is at the heart of teaching and learning. Whether designing curriculum units or laying out instructional plans, teachers make decisions about what to emphasize and what must sit by the wayside. How do we make cogent and meaningful choices about what is core for our learners? How can we have confidence in our instructional sequences so that our students forge a pathway to the core?

These questions take on even more significance with the advent of the Common Core State Standards, as schools and districts dive into unwrapping, scaffolding, and integrating these standards directly into their practice. While we seek guidance on how to address these new standards, we simultaneously wish to adhere to what we know works—the finest of proven teaching methodology.

In your hands, you hold a genuine edu-toolkit loaded with clear, specific strategies to help you and your colleagues address key Common Core–related challenges at all grade levels. Based on years of field experience and action research, Harvey Silver, Thomas Dewing, and Matthew Perini have shaped an eminently practical book focused on six core practices that students need to cultivate to become independent learners. The six strategies clearly address the CCSS, but they do more than that. Given that these Core Six impact lifelong learning, they directly support the mission of the architects of the Common Core to provide the basis for college and career readiness. The Core Six are

1. Reading for Meaning.

2. Compare & Contrast.

3. Inductive Learning.

4. Circle of Knowledge.

5. Write to Learn.

6. Vocabulary's CODE.

With these Core Six, the authors have taken the candid and refreshing point of view that you have already steeped yourself in the Common Core State Standards and are fully aware of the importance of this national initiative. Rather than providing a primer on the Common Core, the authors show how six essential strategies can provide a central focus for faculties, a common ground for schoolwide efforts to improve performance and increase student engagement.

Each core strategy is unpacked and revealed through examples for classroom practice with suggested phases, questions, and activities to assist any teacher in any subject. The book is loaded with charts, activity excerpts, images, and text features that make it easy for all teachers to implement the strategies. At the same time, creative teachers will be able to tweak and build on these numerous examples for adaptation in the classroom.

Most important, these Core Six are for our learners. The only person who can improve his or her performance is the individual student. We cannot do it for our students. Our task is to coach them, direct them, and support them so that they know how to assess and improve their own work. To do this well, students need strategies. I believe that these Core Six can easily be translated from teaching strategies to learning strategies for today's students—learning strategies that can be directly fused with 21st century tools and contexts. With the Core Six under their belts, students will be better equipped to tackle the challenges of the future.

Silver, Dewing, and Perini have a spectacular track record of giving educators throughout the world approaches, strategies, and ways of thinking to reach learners and collaborate effectively. With *The Core Six,* the authors have generated another rich contribution to the field, helping us to make astute and critical choices about what should be core in our classrooms.

Acknowledgments

We gratefully acknowledge the contributions of Justin Gilbert. Justin did the hardest job of all: he got the three of us to move, and he brought coherence to our chaos. We would also like to thank the talented and thoughtful team at ASCD. Special thanks go to Genny Ostertag, David Hargis, and Miriam Goldstein.

Finally, we are thankful for Heidi Hayes Jacobs, who lent her distinctive voice and passion to this book's foreword within an almost impossible time frame. Heidi has a rare gift for connecting what's new in education to what's always been true about good teaching and learning.

Introducing the Core Six

Let's begin with what this book is *not*. This book is not a guide to the Common Core State Standards. In it, you will not find the story of how the Common Core emerged, a detailed description of what the standards cover, or an explanation of how the standards are organized. For this information, we recommend visiting the Common Core website (www.corestandards.org) or, for a deeper look, reading John Kendall's (2011) *Understanding Common Core State Standards*.

The Core Six is for educators who already have a strong grasp on the Common Core and are eager to do something about it. In this book, we offer a collection of research-based strategies that will help teachers and students respond to the demands of the Common Core, particularly the *Common Core State Standards for English Language Arts & Literacy in History/ Social Studies, Science, and Technical Subjects*, which are a "shared responsibility within the school" (National Governors Association Center for Best Practices [NGA Center], Council of Chief State School Officers [CCSSO], 2010a, p. 4) and affect every subject area and grade level.

Regular use of the strategies in this book will help students become better at

- Reading and understanding rigorous texts.
- Evaluating evidence and using it to support positions.
- Conducting comparative analyses.
- Finding important patterns and structures built into content.
- Mastering academic vocabulary and integrating it into speech and writing.

- Understanding and contributing to meaningful discussions about content.
- Using writing to advance learning and clarify thinking.
- Writing comfortably in the key Common Core text types: arguments, informative/explanatory texts, and narratives.

Figure I.1 describes each of the six strategies offered in this book and highlights some of the Common Core skills that each strategy builds.

Making Research Work

Thanks to more than 40 years of research on classroom practice, we know better than ever what works. We know which strategies are likely to increase engagement and raise student achievement, and we know which are not worthy of instructional time. Every strategy in this book is backed by a strong research base.

But research is only part of the story. There is a real gap between research and practice, and any strategy can fall flat in the classroom. Take Compare & Contrast, a strategy that extensive research has found correlates with sizeable gains in student achievement. Ask a few hundred teachers about Compare & Contrast, however, and you will likely get a different take. We actually *did* ask a few hundred teachers about their experiences with Compare & Contrast and learned why a strategy with such a rich research base often fails and how to make classroom comparisons powerful and effective. Here's the gist: if you want to get results, you need to treat Compare & Contrast as a learning strategy rather than an end-of-learning assessment; make sure students have clear criteria for comparing items; and guide students to deeper thinking in phases.

When teachers make moves like these, student learning takes off. The promise of the research is realized. That's why, during the last 35 years, we have worked with thousands of teachers who have helped us test and refine strategies so that they are not only research-based but also classroom-proven. This holds true for every strategy in this book: all of them have been refined over time with the intent of making research come to life in the classroom.

FIGURE I.1	The Core Six

Reading for Meaning helps students develop the skills that proficient readers use to make sense of rigorous texts. The strategy helps build these Common Core skills:
- Managing text complexity.
- Evaluating and using evidence.
- Developing the core skills of reading (e.g., finding main ideas, making inferences, and analyzing characters and content).

Compare & Contrast teaches students to conduct a thorough comparative analysis. The strategy helps build these Common Core skills:
- Conducting comparative analyses of academic content (e.g., renewable versus nonrenewable energy).
- Conducting comparative readings of two or more texts.
- Integrating information from multiple sources.

Inductive Learning helps students find patterns and structures built into content through an inductive process (analyzing specifics to form generalizations). The strategy helps build these Common Core skills:
- Finding patterns and making logical inferences.
- Supporting thinking with evidence.
- Mastering academic vocabulary.

Circle of Knowledge is a strategic framework for planning and conducting classroom discussions that engage all students in deeper thinking and thoughtful communication. The strategy helps build these Common Core skills:
- Speaking, listening, and presenting.
- Integrating and evaluating information.
- Collaborating with peers.

Write to Learn helps teachers integrate writing into daily instruction and develop students' writing skills in the key text types associated with college and career readiness. The strategy helps build these Common Core skills:
- Developing higher-order thinking through writing.
- Writing in the key Common Core text types: arguments, informative/explanatory texts, and narratives.
- Writing for a wide range of tasks, audiences, and purposes.

Vocabulary's CODE is a strategic approach to vocabulary instruction that improves students' ability to retain and use crucial vocabulary terms. The strategy helps build these Common Core skills:
- Mastering academic vocabulary.
- Improving literacy across all strands (reading, writing, speaking/listening, and language).
- Building background knowledge as a foundation for success in school, college, and career.

Six Tips for Inspired Instruction

Even a strategy that has been refined through classroom use is not a magic bullet; it won't increase student engagement or learning on its own. What's more, if you treat a strategy as a list of steps to follow, then the learning you get back will be similarly prosaic. To ensure that your work in strategic instruction is inspired rather than tired, we offer the following six tips.

1. Capture students' interest. Both common sense and research tell us that when students are engaged in what they are learning, their achievement increases (Fredricks, Blumenfeld, & Paris, 2004; Marzano, 2007). Whenever you begin a lesson, you will experience better results if you take the time to design a good "hook." A hook is a question or an activity that provokes student thinking and activates prior knowledge related to the content to come. A well-designed hook will establish a strong sense of intrigue or curiosity at the lesson's outset. To design an attention-grabbing hook, try using

- *Mystery.* On paper, the U.S. Civil War was a mismatch. So why did it last for more than four years? Generate some ideas.

- *Controversy.* Look at these famous masterpieces of modern art. Some use only basic shapes or a single color. Is this really art? What is art?

- *Personal experiences.* Have you ever felt so guilty about something that you thought others could tell you did something wrong just by looking at you? How can guilt be like a stain?

- *"What if" questions.* What if there were no plants? How might the world be different?

Hooks can also focus on the specific strategy you'll be using. For example, if you're about to introduce the Compare & Contrast strategy, you might ask students to think about a time they had to compare two or more things to make a good decision.

After students have collected and shared their ideas, bridge the discussion to the lesson: "Good! You have come up with some great examples of how we use comparison in our everyday lives. Now, let's learn how we can make our comparative thinking even stronger using the Compare & Contrast strategy."

2. Explain the strategy's purpose and students' roles in the strategy. Students don't come to school with a strategy gene. Strategic thinking does not usually come naturally. Whenever you use a strategy, take the time to tell students its name and explain how it works and why it is important. Most essential, teach students the specific steps in the strategy and explain what you expect them to do at each step. Research (Brown, Pressley, Van Meter, & Schuder, 1996) shows that explicitly teaching the steps and making expectations clear enable students to use strategies independently. One highly effective tool for teaching strategies directly to students is a classroom poster. Figure I.2 shows a classroom poster delineating the steps of the Reading for Meaning strategy (Silver, Morris, & Klein, 2010).

FIGURE I.2   Reading for Meaning Classroom Poster

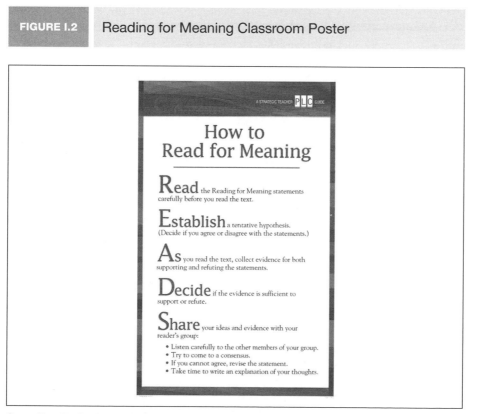

Source: From *Reading for Meaning: How to Build Students' Comprehension, Reasoning, and Problem-Solving Skills (A Strategic Teacher PLC Guide)*, by H. F. Silver, S. C. Morris, and V. Klein, 2010, Alexandria, VA: ASCD. © 2010 Silver Strong & Associates/Thoughtful Education Press. Reprinted with permission.

3. Teach the thinking embedded in the strategy. For example, collecting and evaluating evidence is one crucial thinking skill embedded in several Core Six strategies. To teach this skill, discuss the concept of *evidence* with students. What is evidence? When and how is it used? What's the difference between an argument that uses evidence and one that doesn't? Model what good evidence sounds like using simple claims like "Taking care of a pet is harder than taking care of a plant." Whenever students make a claim during a lesson, use it as an opportunity to explore the evidence behind the claim.

4. Use discussion and questioning techniques to extend student thinking. To move students from superficial to deep understanding, extend student thinking through questioning and discussion. A simple but powerful technique for improving classroom questioning and discussion is Q-SPACE (Strong, Hanson, & Silver, 1998), a strategy described fully on page 42.

5. Ask students to synthesize and transfer their learning. Challenge students to pull together what they have learned and transfer that learning to a new context. For example, after completing a Circle of Knowledge discussion in which 5th grade students debate a local issue (should their small town allow a big-box store to build on a vacant lot?), you might present three more debatable issues for students to discuss in teams, using what they have learned about civil debate and compromise to resolve each issue.

6. Leave time for reflection. When using a strategy, students need time to think back not only on the content but also on the process. For example, you might say, "Let's think back on our use of 3 x 3 Writing Frames [a tool that's part of the Write to Learn strategy]. How did the 3 x 3 Writing Frame help you plan your essay? What might you do differently next time you use a 3 x 3 Writing Frame?"

1
Reading for Meaning

Reading for Meaning in a Nutshell

Reading for Meaning is a research-based strategy that helps all readers build the skills that proficient readers use to make sense of challenging texts. Regular use of the strategy gives students the opportunity to practice and master the three phases of critical reading that lead to reading success, including

- Previewing and predicting *before reading.*
- Actively searching for relevant information *during reading.*
- Reflecting on learning *after reading.*

Three Reasons for Using Reading for Meaning to Address the Common Core

1. Text complexity. Reading Anchor Standard 10 and Appendix A in the Common Core State Standards for ELA & Literacy (NGA Center & CCSSO, 2010a) both call for increasing the complexity of the texts that students are expected to be able to read as they progress through school. Reading for Meaning builds in all students the skills used by proficient readers to extract meaning from even the most rigorous texts.

2. Evidence. The Common Core's Reading Anchor Standard 1 and Writing Anchor Standards 1 and 9 all highlight the vital role of evidence in supporting thinking. As the English Language Arts standards' (NGA Center & CCSSO, 2010a) description of college and career readiness states, "Students cite specific evidence when offering an oral or written interpretation of a text. They use relevant evidence when supporting their own points in writing and speaking, making their reasoning clear to the reader or listener, and they constructively evaluate others' use of evidence" (p. 7). Few strategies put a greater premium on evidence than Reading for Meaning, which provides direct, supported training in how to find, assess, and use relevant textual evidence.

3. The core skills of reading. Reading for Meaning helps teachers build and assess the exact skills that the Common Core identifies as crucial to students' success, including identifying main ideas, making inferences, and supporting interpretations with evidence. Because Reading for Meaning uses teacher-created statements to guide students' reading, teachers can easily craft statements to address any of the Common Core's standards for reading. See Figure 1.2 (p. 14) to learn how you can design statements to address different anchor standards.

The Research Behind Reading for Meaning

Reading for Meaning is deeply informed by a line of research known as *comprehension instruction*. Some scholars attribute the beginning of the comprehension instruction movement to Dolores Durkin's (1978/1979) study "What Classroom Observations Reveal About Reading Comprehension Instruction." Durkin discovered that most teachers were setting students up for failure by making the false assumption that comprehension—the very thing students were being tested on—did not need to be taught. As long as students were reading the words correctly and fluently, teachers assumed that they were "getting it."

Thanks in part to Durkin's findings, a new generation of researchers began investigating the hidden skills and cognitive processes that underlie reading comprehension. A number of researchers (see, for example, Pressley & Afflerbach, 1995; Wyatt et al., 1993) focused their attention on a simple but unexplored question: What do great readers do when they read? By studying the behaviors of skilled readers, these researchers reached some important conclusions about what it takes to read for meaning, including these three:

1. **Good reading is active reading.** Pressley (2006) observed, "In general, the conscious processing that is excellent reading begins before reading, continues during reading, and persists after reading is completed" (p. 57). Thus, good readers are actively engaged not only *during* reading but also *before* reading (when they call up what they already know about the topic and establish a purpose for reading) and *after* reading (when they reflect on and seek to deepen their understanding).

2. **Comprehension involves a repertoire of skills, or reading and thinking strategies.** Zimmermann and Hutchins (2003) synthesize the findings of the research on proficient readers by identifying "seven keys to comprehension," a set of skills that includes making connections to background knowledge, drawing inferences, and determining importance.

3. **These comprehension skills can be taught successfully to nearly all readers, including young and emerging readers.** In *Mosaic of Thought* (2007), Keene and Zimmermann show how teachers at all grade levels teach comprehension skills in their classrooms. What's more, a wide body of research shows that teaching students comprehension skills has "a significant and lasting effect on students' understanding" (Keene, 2010, p. 70).

Reading for Meaning is designed around these research findings. The strategy breaks reading into three phases (before, during, and after reading) and develops in students of all ages the processing skills they need during each phase to build deep understanding.

Implementing Reading for Meaning in the Classroom

1. Identify a short text that you want students to "read for meaning." Any kind of text is fine—a poem, an article, a blog post, a primary document, a fable, or a scene from a play. Mathematical word problems, data charts, and visual sources like paintings and photographs also work well. The "Other Considerations" section of this chapter (p. 15) provides more details on nontextual applications.

2. Generate a list of statements about the text. Students will ultimately search the text for evidence that supports or refutes each statement. Statements can be objectively true or false, or they can be open to interpretation and designed to provoke discussion and debate. They can be customized to fit whichever skills, standards, or objectives you're working on—for example, identifying main ideas or analyzing characters and ideas. (See Figure 1.2 on page 14 for details.)

3. Introduce the topic of the text and have students preview the statements *before* they begin reading. Encourage students to think about what they already know about the topic and to use the statements to make some predictions about the text.

4. Have students record evidence for and against each statement *while* (or *after*) they read.

5. Have students discuss their evidence in pairs or small groups. Encourage groups to reach consensus about which statements are supported and which are refuted by the text. If they are stuck, have them rewrite any problematic statements in a way that enables them to reach consensus.

6. Conduct a whole-class discussion in which students share and justify their positions. If necessary, help students clarify their thinking and call their attention to evidence that they might have missed or misinterpreted.

7. Use students' responses to evaluate their understanding of the reading and their ability to support a position with evidence.

Reading for Meaning Sample Lessons

Sample Lesson 1: Primary English Language Arts

Erin Rohmer introduces her 1st graders to the concept of evidence by posing this statement: "First grade is harder than kindergarten." After finding that all her students agree with the statement, Erin asks students why they agree: "What are you being asked to do this year in school that you didn't have to do last year? What new things are you learning that are more challenging than what you learned last year?"

As Erin collects students' ideas, she explains that the reasons and examples they are coming up with are *evidence,* or information that helps prove an idea. Erin goes on to explain that the class will be practicing the skill of collecting evidence from a story.

Today, the class is reading Janet Stevens's (1995) *Tops & Bottoms,* a story about a clever hare who tricks a lazy bear. For this initial use of Reading for Meaning, Erin asks students to consider just one statement: "The hare deceived the bear." Notice how Erin is helping students master an important and challenging vocabulary term—*deceive*—with this statement. After clarifying the meaning of the new vocabulary word with students, Erin reads the story aloud while students follow along. Students stop Erin whenever they find information in the story that seems to support or refute the statement. The class discusses each piece of evidence together and decides whether it helps prove or disprove the statement. Erin records students' ideas on an interactive whiteboard using the organizer shown in Figure 1.1.

FIGURE 1.1   Support/Refute Organizer for *Tops & Bottoms*

Evidence For	Statement	Evidence Against
	The hare deceived the bear. (Remember: deceive means <u>to trick</u>.)	

After finishing the story, Erin asks students to work in small groups to review the assembled evidence and then to nominate the three best pieces of evidence from the organizer. As the groups work together, Erin listens in to assess students' emerging ability to evaluate evidence.

Sample Lesson 2: Elementary Mathematics

Note: The following sample lesson has been adapted from Reading for Meaning: How to Build Students' Comprehension, Reasoning, and Problem-Solving Skills *(Silver, Morris, & Klein, 2010).*

Third grade teacher Heather Alvarez uses Reading for Meaning statements to help her students analyze and think their way through mathematical word problems before, during, and after the problem-solving process. First, she poses the problem: "Most 3rd graders get their hair cut four times a year. Human hair grows at a rate of about 0.5 inches a month. If you get 2 inches of hair cut off during a year, about how much longer will your hair be at the end of that year?"

Heather then asks students to decide whether they agree or disagree with these statements before they begin solving the problem:

1. The first sentence contains relevant information. (This statement is designed to build students' skills in separating relevant from irrelevant information.)

2. Human hair grows at a rate of 1 inch every two months. (This statement is designed to focus attention on the central information.)

3. To solve this problem, you need to find out how much hair grows in a year. (This statement is designed to help students expose hidden questions.)

4. You need to do only one operation to solve this problem. (This statement is designed to help students think through the steps in solving the problem.)

Students review the statements again after solving the problem to see how the problem-solving process challenged or confirmed their initial thinking.

Sample Lesson 3: Middle School Science

Directions: As we work through this lesson, I will be showing you some computer simulations on the whiteboard. You will be asked to collect evidence for and/or against each of these possible conclusions:

1. Most of the volume of an atom is empty space.

2. The electrons orbit the nucleus of an atom in much the same way that planets orbit the sun.

3. A carbon atom is more complex than a helium atom.

4. Most of the atomic mass of an atom comes from its electrons.

Planning Considerations

To develop a Reading for Meaning lesson, think about what you will need to do to introduce the lesson and to prepare for each phase of the lesson.

- Begin by asking yourself, "What standards do I intend to address?"

- After you select the reading for your lesson, ask yourself, "What article, document, or passage needs emphasis and intensive analysis? How will this reading help me address my chosen standards?"

- To analyze the reading, ask yourself, "What themes, main ideas, and details do my students need to discover?"

- To develop Reading for Meaning statements, ask yourself, "What thought-provoking statements can I present to my students before they begin reading to focus and engage their attention? How can I use different kinds of statements to help my students build crucial reading skills found in the Common Core?"

- To decide how to begin the lesson, ask yourself, "What kind of hook, or attention-grabbing question or activity, can I create to capture student interest and activate prior knowledge at the outset of the lesson?"

- To develop leading questions that provoke discussion, ask yourself, "What questions about the content or the process can I develop to engage my students in a discussion throughout the lesson and after the reading?"

Crafting Reading for Meaning Statements to Address Common Core State Standards

Figure 1.2 shows how you can design Reading for Meaning statements to address specific Anchor Standards for Reading.

FIGURE 1.2	Aligning Reading for Meaning Statements to Anchor Standards

Anchor Standard Concepts	Sample Statements
Determine what a text says explicitly. (R.CCR.1)	• Everyone is unkind to Little Bear. • Animals prepare for winter in different ways.
Make logical inferences from a text. (R.CCR.1)	• We can tell that Pooh and Piglet have been friends for a long time. • Without taking Franklin's data, Watson and Crick wouldn't have succeeded.
Identify main ideas and themes. (R.CCR.2)	• The moral of the story is that teams can do more than individuals. • Structure and function are intricately linked.
Analyze how and why individuals, events, and ideas develop, connect, and interact. (R.CCR.3)	• Pickles goes from being a bad cat to a good cat. • After Maxim's revelation, the new Mrs. de Winter is a changed woman. • The seeds of social change for women in America were planted during WWII.
Assess how point of view or purpose shapes the content and style of a text; distinguish between what is said and what is meant or true. (R.CCR.6)	• Chekhov wants us to judge Julia harshly. • The writer's personal feelings influenced his description of this event.
Integrate and evaluate content that is presented visually and quantitatively as well as in words. (R.CCR.7)	• Munch's *The Scream* shares many stylistic elements with Impressionism. • According to the table in this article, sun worshippers would be happier living in Phoenix than in Seattle.
Analyze how two or more texts address similar themes or topics in order to build knowledge or compare the authors' approaches. (R.CCR.9)	• The two fables we read are more similar than different. • The Cherokee people's account of their relocation differs from the account in your textbook.

Source: Adapted from *Tools for Thoughtful Assessment*, by A. L. Boutz, H. F. Silver, J. W. Jackson, and M. J. Perini, 2012, Ho-Ho-Kus, NJ: Thoughtful Education Press. © 2012 Silver Strong & Associates/Thoughtful Education Press. Used with permission.

Writing Extension: Written Arguments

Use a Reading for Meaning statement to help students develop the kinds of written arguments called for in the Common Core (W.CCR.1). The statement can come from a completed Reading for Meaning lesson, or you can introduce a new one. Either way, the statement should sit at the center of the content, tie back to your instructional objectives, and require students to draw heavily on the text to make their case. A 3 x 3 Writing Frame is a great tool to help students plan and structure arguments because it makes clear what the beginning, middle, and end of their arguments need to contain. It also helps students communicate their ideas with the kind of clarity and precision that define careful thinkers. Figure 5.1 (p. 58) shows how an elementary school student used a 3 x 3 Writing Frame to plan an argument essay on Harriet Tubman.

Other Considerations: Almost Everything Can Be "Read" for Meaning

Although Reading for Meaning has the word *reading* in its name, its use is not limited to texts. The strategy works well with any information source—data charts, paintings, film clips, websites, lab experiments, and so on—because it forces students to analyze information closely and justify their interpretations with evidence. For example, an elementary school teacher asked students to analyze a data table showing the average monthly temperatures and precipitation amounts for various cities throughout the world. To help students build their data-analysis skills, she asked them to use the data from the chart to either support or refute these statements:

1. London receives more precipitation in a year than Vancouver.

2. Over the course of the year, Warsaw sees more snow than rain.

3. On average, January is the coldest month among all the cities.

4. If you were spending Independence Day in Philadelphia, the temperature would probably not be above 87°F.

2
Compare & Contrast

Compare & Contrast in a Nutshell

Compare & Contrast is a critical thinking strategy designed to build students' memories, eliminate confusion, and bring crucial similarities and differences into sharp focus. The strategy maximizes the effectiveness of the natural human capacity to make comparisons by guiding students through a four-phase learning process: first, students describe each item using criteria; second, they use a Top Hat Organizer to record key similarities and differences; third, they discuss their findings and draw conclusions; and finally, they synthesize their learning by completing an application task.

Three Reasons for Using Compare & Contrast to Address the Common Core

1. Comparative thinking. Search the Common Core, and you will find dozens of grade-specific standards (e.g., RL.K.9, RL.7.7, RI.4.6, RI.6.9, W.5.9a, L.5.3b, RH.9-10.9, RST.6-8.9, K.CC.7, 2.NBT.4, 3.NF.3d, 4.NF.2, 8.F.2, F-IF.9, S-IC.5) that require students to think comparatively. Compare & Contrast teaches students to conduct careful and thoughtful comparative analyses in four steps.

2. Comparative reading. When applied specifically to reading, Compare & Contrast develops students' abilities to read two texts against each other, draw out common themes, and identify the most salient differences, a skill that gets its very own Anchor Standard: "Analyze how two or more texts address similar themes or topics in order to build knowledge or to compare the approaches the authors take" (R.CCR.9).

3. A "best bet" for raising student achievement. One reason comparative thinking gets so much emphasis in the Common Core State Standards is that the research behind it is compelling. In *Classroom Instruction That Works*, for example, Marzano, Pickering, and Pollock (2001) identify comparative thinking strategies as the single most effective way to raise student achievement. Note, however, that these gains come only when such strategies are used well. Compare & Contrast provides students with a replicable process that enables them to conduct deep and meaningful comparisons both in the classroom and on their own.

The Research Behind Compare & Contrast

The research behind comparison in the classroom is eye opening, with multiple meta-studies (Dean, Hubbell, Pitler, & Stone, 2012; Marzano, 2007; Marzano et al., 2001) showing that the strategy leads to significant gains in student achievement. Yet many teachers have used comparison in the classroom and not seen the results the research promises. What gives?

To find out, we worked with teachers and students to identify the most common reasons comparisons fail in the classroom. In this section, we describe these pitfalls and explain how the Compare & Contrast strategy enables teachers to sidestep them.

Pitfall 1: Teachers use comparisons *after* learning, as either test items or end-of-chapter questions. This emphasis on evaluation reinforces students' sense that comparison is about finding the right answer rather than about discovery and analysis. Because it is a learning strategy, not an assessment strategy, Compare & Contrast requires teachers to provide a clear purpose for the lesson. For example, "People often confuse *meiosis* and *mitosis*. Let's compare them to make sure we're clear about what they have in common and how they differ."

Pitfall 2: Students rush into the comparison before they know the characteristics of what they are comparing. To avoid this pitfall, Compare & Contrast begins with a description phase in which students use rich information sources to identify essential attributes of the items before comparing them. For example, "Use the two readings to help you develop a clear description of renewable and nonrenewable energy."

Pitfall 3: Students don't know what to look for. Any two objects can be compared in multiple ways. Which aspects are important? How will students know when they are done? Compare & Contrast requires teachers to provide clear criteria that keep students focused on the relevant information. For example, "As you describe FDR and Winston Churchill, focus on what made each leader unique, the challenges each faced, and what each accomplished."

Pitfall 4: Students don't have an efficient way to visualize similarities and differences. The most common comparison organizer, the Venn Diagram, leaves too little space to write in the middle, and the presence of the similarities in the middle prevents students from lining up parallel differences. Compare & Contrast uses a Top Hat Organizer (see Figure 2.1) that gives students sufficient space to record similarities and enables them to record parallel differences directly across from each other.

FIGURE 2.1	Student's Top Hat Organizer for the U.S. Congress

House of Representatives	Senate
Serve for two years	Serve for six years
435 representatives	100 senators
Number of representatives depends on each state's population	Each state has two senators
Led by the Speaker of the House	Led by the Vice President of the United States

Similarities
The House and Senate make up the legislative branch of government.
Both propose and debate legislation.

Pitfall 5: Teachers treat the identification of similarities and differences as the end of the comparison process. Instead of comparing and contrasting two items and leaving it at that, Compare & Contrast uses higher-order questions to help students draw conclusions and extend their thinking about the significance of key similarities and differences. For example,

- Are reptiles and amphibians more alike or more different? Defend your position.

- What do you think is the most important difference between the two speeches we read?

- Based on your comparison of expressions and equations, what conclusions can you draw?

- A significant difference between an autobiography and a biography is the author. What effect does this difference have on the reader?

Pitfall 6: Students don't apply or transfer their learning. To sidestep this pitfall, Compare & Contrast includes a synthesis task that challenges students to put their learning to use in a meaningful way. For example, "Now that you've compared problems that ask you to solve for rate with problems that ask you to solve for time, I want you to create and solve two new problems. One should require you to solve for rate, and one should require you to solve for time. Then create a third problem that requires you to solve for distance."

Implementing Compare & Contrast in the Classroom

To maximize the power of comparative thinking, Compare & Contrast moves through four implementation phases in the classroom.

Phase One: Description

- Begin with a hook that helps students activate prior knowledge about the topic. Then bridge the discussion from the hook to the purpose of the lesson. For example, "You really know a lot about volume and surface area! Today, we are going to compare the two to make sure we're clear on what they are, how each is calculated and expressed, and when each is used."

- Provide clear criteria to focus student description. A simple three-column organizer is helpful (see Figure 2.2).
- Remind students that their job is to describe each item separately, *not* to compare them. Model as necessary.

FIGURE 2.2	Description Organizer for Volume and Surface Area

Volume	Criteria	Surface Area
	Definition How it's calculated How it's expressed (units) When it's used	

Phase Two: Comparison

- Ask students to use their descriptions and criteria from phase one to search for important similarities and differences. Consider modeling good comparative thinking using everyday objects, such as *fork* and *spoon*.
- Provide a Top Hat Organizer (see Figure 2.1) that enables students to line up parallel differences.

Phase Three: Conclusion

Stretch students' minds and help them draw conclusions by building discussion around concluding questions, such as

- Are the two items more alike or more different?

- What is the most important difference? Think of some causes and effects of this difference.

- What conclusions can you draw?

Phase Four: Application

- Ask students to apply their learning by creating a product or completing a task.

- Over time, move students toward independence by teaching them how to formulate criteria, describe items, determine key similarities and differences, and reflect on their learning.

Compare & Contrast Sample Lessons

Sample Lesson 1: Primary English Language Arts

Note: The following sample lesson has been adapted from Compare & Contrast: Teaching Comparative Thinking to Strengthen Student Learning *(Silver, 2010).*

Description phase. As part of a unit on American tall tales, Gabby Sanzo is reading the tales of Paul Bunyan and Pecos Bill with her 2nd graders. Gabby begins by working with students to define *exaggeration* and asks students to share some experiences in which they or someone they know exaggerated. Then Gabby poses the hook: "Why do people exaggerate?" After collecting students' ideas, Gabby explains that they are going to be reading a kind of story called a *tall tale* that uses exaggeration to make the characters seem bigger or more powerful than ordinary people.

Gabby first reads the two tall tales aloud as students follow along. Then, as students read on their own, she helps them collect information from each tall tale using three questions:

1. What is the character like? (values/personality)

2. What is the setting like?

3. How is the character exaggerated?

Comparison phase. Next, Gabby has students use the information they collected to identify the similarities and differences between the two tall tales. Gabby shows her students how to record this information on a Top Hat Organizer.

Conclusion phase. For the discussion, Gabby poses this question: "Are the two tales more similar or more different?" After a few minutes of discussion, Gabby asks students to speculate as to why the heroes of tall tales might be exaggerated by their authors.

Application phase. To help her students synthesize what they have learned, Gabby asks them to think about superheroes. Together, Gabby and her students come up with some ideas about what superheroes do and their powers/abilities. Gabby then writes, "The heroes in tall tales are like today's superheroes" on the board. She helps her students generate some ideas about how the statement might be interpreted as true or false before asking them to write a one-paragraph "I think" essay. Student essays must begin with either "I think the heroes in tall tales are like today's superheroes" or "I think the heroes in tall tales are not like today's superheroes."

Sample Lesson 2: Upper-Elementary/ Middle School Mathematics

Description phase. Alison Wilder wants to help her students recognize important patterns in mathematical problem solving. Today, she presents two problems to students. Although both problems involve discounts and percentages, each problem has a different unknown, and each needs to be set up and solved differently.

Problem A: I bought a mountain bike that was on sale for $250. During the sale, the store offered a 10% discount. How much money did I save?

Problem B: I bought a jacket that was on sale. At a 10% discount, I ended up saving $6. What was the original price?

Students analyze and describe each problem using these criteria: What is the unknown in the problem? What equation should you use to solve the problem? What's the solution to the problem? As students complete their descriptions and solve each problem, Alison circulates around the room to get a reading on students' abilities to recognize the patterns in each problem.

Comparison phase. After students have described and solved the problems, Alison reviews to make sure all students understand how each problem is solved. Next, students use a Top Hat Organizer to identify the essential similarities and differences between the problems.

Key similarities students note include

- Something is purchased.
- The original price is discounted.
- An amount is saved.

Key differences students note include

- In Problem A, we're looking for the savings. In Problem B, we're looking for the original price.
- In Problem A's equation, N is by itself. In Problem B's equation, N is with another number.
- For Problem A, we follow the equation. For Problem B, we change the equation.
- For Problem A, we multiply the original price by the discount to get the savings. For Problem B, we divide the savings by the discount to get the original price.

Conclusion phase. To help students draw conclusions about patterns in problem solving, Alison presents two more problems. Students must explain which problem is like Problem A and which is like Problem B.

Problem C: Samantha bought a dress. She saved $6. The discount was 12%. What was the original price of the dress?

Problem D: Steve wanted to buy a pack of vintage baseball cards, but the price of $80 was too high. The dealer agreed to give Steve a 20% discount. How much would Steve save?

Application phase. Alison presents one more problem to students. The problem does not fit exactly with the two types of problems they have solved so far. In addition to solving the problem, students must decide which type of problem it resembles more and explain why.

Problem E: Steve and Sally bought their mother a new tennis racket on sale. It originally cost $80, but the sale price saves them $24. What percentage discount did they receive?

Sample Lesson 3: High School Social Studies

Description phase. As part of their yearlong investigation of great debates in American history, students in Mercer Kaleen's class are learning about Booker T. Washington and W. E. B. Du Bois. Students read about and discuss these two great African American leaders and their opposing views on how to achieve racial equality. They collect key information in a Description Organizer using three criteria: each leader's accomplishments, each leader's views on the purpose of education, and each leader's goals for social change.

Comparison phase. After describing each leader, students use a Top Hat Organizer to identify important similarities and differences.

Conclusion phase. Mercer discusses with students the question "Whose position do you find more persuasive, and why?"

Application phase. To help students apply their learning and see how debates in history reverberate through time, Mercer asks his students to read a brief newspaper editorial about the funding crisis facing career and technical education programs. Students must assume the perspective of either Washington or Du Bois and respond to the editorial.

Planning Considerations

To develop a Compare & Contrast lesson, think about what you will need to do to introduce the lesson and to prepare for each phase of the lesson.

- Begin by asking yourself, "What standards do I intend to address?"
- To define your purpose, ask yourself, "Why am I engaging students in this comparison? What insights do I want students to gain?" Make sure you clearly explain the purpose to students when you implement the lesson.
- When selecting content, ask yourself, "What paired concepts or texts will naturally heighten understanding when considered together?"

- To plan phase one (description), ask yourself, "What sources of information will students use? What criteria will students use to describe both items?"

- To plan phase two (comparison), ask yourself, "How will I introduce and model the use of the Top Hat Organizer?"

- To plan phase three (conclusion), ask yourself, "How will I facilitate discussion and help students draw conclusions?" Good discussion questions that help students draw conclusions include

  — Are the two items more alike or more different?
  — What is the most important difference between the two?
  — What are the possible reasons for this difference?
  — What can you conclude from your comparison?

- To plan phase four (application), ask yourself, "What kind of task can I give to students that will enable them to demonstrate and transfer their learning in a meaningful way?"

Writing Extension: Comparative Essays

Comparative essays are among the most common essay forms and are featured prominently in the Common Core. The Compare & Contrast strategy gives you a natural opportunity to work with students to convert their comparisons into clear comparative essays. Teach them how to use the following transitional words and phrases associated with comparing and contrasting:

Alike	Have in common	Nonetheless
Although	However	Not only...but also
But	In contrast to	On the other hand
Compared with	Less than	Similar to
Different from	More than	While
Either...or	Neither...nor	Yet

Students—especially younger students—developing their first few comparison essays will benefit from a simple writing framework like the one shown in Figure 2.3 (p. 26), which provides a clear structure for communicating their ideas with clarity and precision.

FIGURE 2.3	Comparative Writing Framework

I am comparing and contrasting _____ and _____.

Although _____ and _____ are different, they are alike

in some ways. For example, _____ and _____

are both _____. There are also some interesting differences between

_____ and _____. For example, _____

_____.

[Concluding sentence:] _____.

Other Considerations: The Many Ways to Compare

At the heart of Compare & Contrast lies one of the most essential skills needed for academic success: the ability to differentiate between items in terms of their similarities and differences. However, Compare & Contrast is only one strategy for developing this ability. In both editions of *Classroom Instruction That Works* (Dean et al., 2012; Marzano et al., 2001), the authors identify three additional research-based forms this instructional category can take: classifying, creating metaphors, and creating analogies. To see how one of these other forms—classification—works as a research-based strategy, see Chapter 3.

3
Inductive Learning

Inductive Learning in a Nutshell

Inductive Learning is a powerful strategy for helping students deepen their understanding of content and develop their inference and evidence-gathering skills. In an Inductive Learning lesson, students examine, group, and label specific "bits" of information to find patterns. For example, if given 20 specific weather-related terms (e.g., *rain, sleet, snow, hygrometer, rain gauge, thermometer, humid, dry, windy, cold*), students might group the terms into an initial set of categories labeled *precipitation, weather instruments,* and *how weather feels*. Inductive Learning does not stop at categorization, however; it also asks students to use their labeled groups to develop a set of working hypotheses about the content to come. Then, during the learning, students collect evidence to verify or refine each of their hypotheses.

Three Reasons for Using Inductive Learning to Address the Common Core

1. Inference. Marzano (2010) identifies inference as a foundational process that underlies higher-order thinking and 21st century skills. Perhaps this is the reason why the Common Core's very first Reading Anchor Standard (R.CCR.1) requires students to "make logical inferences." The Inductive Learning strategy shines a direct light on inference making by emphasizing the sub-processes that go into it: examining information closely, looking for hidden relationships, generating tentative hypotheses, and drawing conclusions that are not explicitly stated.

2. Evidence. Few themes get more attention in the Common Core than evidence. The English Language Arts standards' description of college and career readiness as well as Standard for Mathematical Practice 3, Reading Anchor Standard 1, Writing Anchor Standards 1 and 9, and numerous additional grade-specific standards all require students to support their thinking with high-quality evidence. In an Inductive Learning lesson, the search for evidence fuels the learning process, as students must actively seek out information to support their hypotheses. They must also collect and consider evidence that runs counter to their hypotheses, a practice that leads to stronger, more refined hypotheses.

3. Academic vocabulary. Because most Inductive Learning lessons are built around words and terms, the strategy is a great way to introduce "academic and domain-specific words and phrases" (L.CCR.6) to students. But Inductive Learning does more than simply introduce new vocabulary terms: it forces students to search for key attributes and relationships among the words, a skill emphasized in Language Anchor Standard 5. Students use the relationships they discover to help them organize all of the terms into a schema that suggests the larger structure of the content.

The Research Behind Inductive Learning

Inductive Learning is based on the pioneering work of educator Hilda Taba (Taba, Durkin, Fraenkel, & McNaughton, 1971). Concerned that education was placing too much emphasis on memorization of discrete facts and not enough emphasis on critical and conceptual thinking, Taba proposed a new instructional approach. In this approach, teachers shift from giving students information to helping students discover the relationships between the big ideas and key details that make up lessons, units, and disciplines. The process encourages students to develop their natural powers of inductive reasoning, moving from specific details to bigger ideas to broad generalizations.

Current research has finally caught up to Taba's inductive-based approach to teaching and learning. New meta-analytical research on effective teaching practices (Dean et al., 2012) suggests that teaching students how to classify information and how to generate and test hypotheses—two core skills built into Taba's model—both raise student achievement.

Implementing Inductive Learning in the Classroom

1. Identify and distribute key words, phrases, items, problems, or images from a reading, lecture, or unit. Note that if you're basing the lesson on words or terms, students will need to assess their understanding of the terms and look up unfamiliar terms.

2. Model the process of grouping and labeling terms.

3. Have students analyze the items and explore the different ways they can group them. Encourage students to think flexibly and to subsume smaller groups into larger, more inclusive groups. Consider having students conduct the grouping process collaboratively, in small teams.

4. Ask students to devise a descriptive label for each of their groups.

5. Have students use their labels and word groupings to make several predictions or hypotheses about the reading, lecture, or unit. As students read the text, listen to the lecture, or participate in the unit, ask them to search for and collect evidence that supports or refutes their predictions. Students should write their predictions on a three-column Support/ Refute Organizer (see Figure 3.2, p. 31), with their hypotheses down the middle column, evidence that supports the hypotheses in the left column, and evidence that refutes the hypotheses in the right column.

6. Ask students to reflect on the Inductive Learning process, and lead a discussion on what they have learned from it.

7. Over time, teach students how to generalize and conceptualize by using the inductive process to identify key words, create groups, generate predictions, and test and refine those predictions against the evidence.

Inductive Learning Sample Lessons

Sample Lesson 1: Middle School U.S. History

Social studies teacher Margaret Shea knows that when students make predictions before reading, their reading becomes more like an inquiry and less like a routine reading assignment. Today, she is using Inductive Learning as part of her unit on pre-colonial Georgia. Using a textbook reading on the people of the Mississippian period (approximately 800 CE–1500 CE),

Margaret selects 25 words and phrases from the reading that support the generalizations she wants students to make. For example, to support the generalization that Mississippian Indians were farmers, Margaret selects a mix of well-known words (*pumpkin*, *squash*, *beans*) and new terms (*digging sticks*, *bone hoes*, *crop rotation*).

Margaret breaks students up into small teams, gives each team a sheet that lists all 25 words, and asks students to cut out the words so that each team has 25 separate pieces of paper. The teams look up unknown terms, create word groups based on common attributes, and devise a descriptive label for each group. Figure 3.1 shows one team's groups and labels.

FIGURE 3.1 Team's Groups and Labels for Mississippian Indians

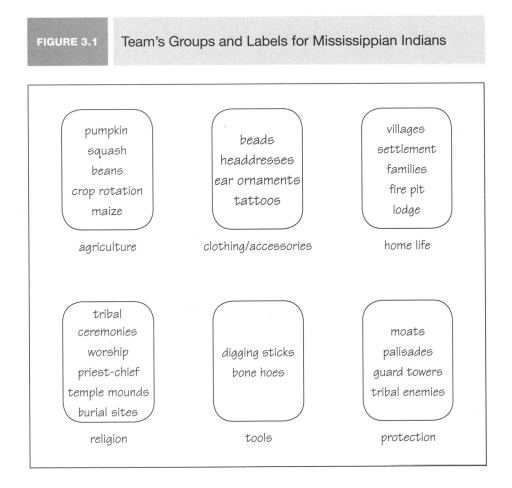

pumpkin
squash
beans
crop rotation
maize

agriculture

beads
headdresses
ear ornaments
tattoos

clothing/accessories

villages
settlement
families
fire pit
lodge

home life

tribal
ceremonies
worship
priest-chief
temple mounds
burial sites

religion

digging sticks
bone hoes

tools

moats
palisades
guard towers
tribal enemies

protection

Each team uses its groups and labels to make three predictions about life during the Mississippian period. Maggie then leads a whole-class discussion to encourage students to share their predictions and explain the reasoning behind them. Each student records his or her three favorite predictions from the discussion in a three-column Support/Refute Organizer (see Figure 3.2).

FIGURE 3.2 Support/Refute Organizer for Mississippian Indians

Evidence For	Prediction	Evidence Against
	Mississippian Indians were farmers.	
	They had more elaborate clothes than the earlier pre-colonial people we learned about.	
	They believed in an afterlife.	

Students use the organizer to read the next section of their textbook. When they come across information that supports one of their predictions, they record it in the "Evidence For" column. When they come across information that runs counter to a prediction, they record it in the "Evidence Against" column.

To encourage students to become more independent as learners, Margaret explains how they can use this process whenever reading becomes difficult. She shows students how to collect words that seem important and group these words to develop a reading framework that helps them see the big ideas.

Sample Lesson 2:
Primary English Language Arts and Social Studies

Don Andre has decided to use Inductive Learning to help his 1st graders discover customs and traditions that families share. A few days earlier,

Don had sent a note home with students asking parents to send in copies of two pictures of their family engaged in various activities.

To begin the lesson, Don places all the pictures in the circle rug area and asks students to look them over carefully. To help students understand the group-and-label process, Don groups pictures based on the clothes the subjects are wearing. Students help him create labels for each group, such as *dress clothes*, *summer clothes*, and so on.

Next, Don tells students, "I want you to look closely at all the pictures and work together to see if you can make at least five different groups based on what the people in the pictures are doing. For each group that we make, we'll need to come up with a label that describes what the pictures in your group all have in common." Sample labels include *holidays, parties, vacations, celebrating achievement,* and *special events*.

After working with the students to create groups and labels, Don writes "Most families…" five times on the board. Don challenges students to use their groups and labels to complete the sentence five different ways.

Once the class has come up with five good sentences, Don reads a story in which a girl meets her friends' various families. Whenever students hear something in the story that relates to one of the sentences on the board, they raise their hands to explain the connection they noticed.

Don synthesizes the lesson by asking students to work in teams to create a set of pictures showing families doing things that most families do. Each team must present and explain its pictures to the class.

Sample Lesson 3: Middle School Science

Middle school science teacher Calvin Brown uses Inductive Learning both to introduce new units and as a review strategy. Currently, students are nearing the end of a unit on cell structure and function. Calvin gives students all 30 vocabulary terms from the unit (including *mitochondria, vacuole, protein, cellulose, excretion, ribosome,* and *replication*) and challenges them to use their knowledge of cellular structure and function to group and label all the terms. Calvin stresses to students that this activity is an opportunity to self-assess their learning and to shore up their understanding of key terms.

Once students have created their groups and labels, Calvin asks them to write a response to this prompt: "Pick three critical functions that cells perform. Explain how the different parts of the cell are involved in each function. Use at least 15 vocabulary terms in your response."

Planning Considerations

To develop an Inductive Learning lesson, think about the standards you expect to address, the deep understandings you want students to develop, how you will introduce the lesson, and how you will help students meet the cognitive demands of the strategy.

- Begin by asking yourself, "What standards do I intend to address? What are the big concepts in this lesson or unit of study that I want students to discover?"

- Select items to group by asking, "What 10–40 items (words, phrases, images, and so on) best represent these concepts?" Remember that students really need three items to make a stable group and that they will have an easier time making sense of new terms if the majority of the terms are familiar to them. Make sure that the items you select are specific, not general. For example, if you want students to discover that religion was important to colonial Americans, use words like *congregation, minister*, and *Sabbath* rather than words like *religion*.

- Establish a way for students to group items by asking yourself, "Will I provide an organizer or have students develop their own organizers?" You should also think about how you will model the grouping-and-labeling process for students who are new to the strategy. Try to model both obvious groupings (e.g., characters in *Romeo and Juliet*) and more subtle ones (e.g., a set of lines from *Romeo and Juliet* that suggests a central theme, such as rivalry).

- To ensure that the lesson runs smoothly, ask yourself, "How will I distribute the items? What is the best way to group students during this lesson?" Make sure that you are able to clearly explain to students what you expect of them during the lesson.

- To deepen understanding, develop some stretching questions to ask students, such as

— What were your thoughts as you made that group?

— If we were to move these items into this group, how would you change the label to accommodate the new items?

— Look at the groups you have made. What do these groupings tell you about what we are going to study?

— Can you form any other groups that we haven't thought about yet?

— Why does this term belong in this group?

- To solidify understanding and promote transfer of learning, ask yourself, "What kind of synthesis task or closing activity can I prepare to help students apply what they have learned?"

Writing Extension: Inductive Writing and Multiple Document Learning

Inductive Writing

Driving the Inductive Learning strategy is a process of grouping and labeling that, once completed, points to a larger organizational structure. This same process can be used to great effect when helping students write multi-paragraph essays. After all, the cognitive processes germane to Inductive Learning—assembling details, determining how those details cluster around bigger ideas, and organizing both the big ideas and the details into an overarching structure—are similar to the cognitive processes involved in essay writing.

Here's how to use Inductive Writing in your classroom.

1. Help students generate ideas related to the topic. For example, if students are writing an informational essay, ask questions that will help them get their background knowledge about the topic out in the open: "What do you know about alligators? What else can you remember? You've got a lot about how alligators look, but can you remember anything about how they behave?"

2. Ask students to look over the words, phrases, and ideas they have generated and then group items together into three or four groups.

3. Ask students to imagine that each group will serve as the basis for a paragraph. Challenge students to create a topic sentence for each group that explains what the paragraph will be about.

4. Ask students to sequence the groups and topic sentences in a way that makes sense. Before students begin writing, give them time to review their groups, add any details that might be missing, revise their topic sentences, and think their way through the essay (How will it open? How will it close? How will one paragraph flow into the next?).

5. Have students produce a first draft.

6. Provide students with opportunities to assess and improve their drafts. For example, you might use the Writer's Club tool (pp. 62–64) to have students work together to refine their essays.

7. Give students time to reflect on the essay-writing process. Pose questions like "What did you learn about how to organize ideas? How did working in a Writer's Club help you? How might you use the Inductive Writing technique for other kinds of writing assignments?"

Multiple Document Learning

In Multiple Document Learning, students use the inductive process to tease out the central themes and important details from two or more documents. This technique is especially useful in the wake of the Common Core reading standards and assessments that require students to "analyze how two or more texts address similar themes or topics" (R.CCR.9).

For example, imagine an assessment that asks students to read three texts: an excerpt of a memoir in which a Chinese student describes her initial experiences in a U.S. school, a description of a classroom during an air-raid drill, and a poem about teaching. Students must discuss how these three texts contribute to their understanding of how teachers help students learn. Here is how you can help students through the process:

1. Ask students to identify the topic embedded in the question (how teachers help students learn).

2. Encourage students to read the texts carefully, looking for any information that relates to the topic. As they read, students should annotate and underline text and make notes to highlight important information.

3. Ask students to review their annotations and notes carefully. What patterns do they see? Encourage them to create a set of groups containing specific information from the texts and give each group a clear label.

4. Have students review their groups and labels. Before they begin writing, give them time to add missing details and clarify their groups.

5. Ask students to set their groups in a logical sequence for writing.

6. As with steps 5–7 in Inductive Writing, have students draft their responses, collaborate to improve their work, and reflect on the process.

4
Circle of Knowledge

Circle of Knowledge in a Nutshell

Despite its enormous importance as a teaching and learning strategy, classroom discussion can be quite fragile. On the one hand, it is highly involving; on the other hand, few strategies suffer as much when students refuse to participate. Classroom discussions help students develop new insights and perspectives, yet they can easily be thrown off track. Learning how to conduct an effective classroom discussion is an essential skill for any teacher to master. Circle of Knowledge provides teachers with a strategic framework for planning and conducting discussions that foster student participation and critical thinking.

Three Reasons for Using Circle of Knowledge to Address the Common Core

1. Effective oral communication is a crucial 21st century skill. It is so crucial, in fact, that it gets its very own strand of Speaking and Listening Standards, along with Reading, Writing, and Language. According to the Common Core, "To become college and career ready, students must have ample opportunities to take part in a variety of rich, structured conversations—as part of a whole class, in small groups, and with a partner—built around important content" (NGA Center & CCSSO, 2010a, p. 48). The Circle of Knowledge strategy helps teachers create a classroom culture where these kinds of "rich, structured conversations" become the norm.

2. Speaking and listening require thinking. A close look at the Standards for Speaking and Listening makes it clear that low-level question-and-answer sessions won't cut it. Students need to be able to "participate effectively…building on others' ideas" (SL.CCR.1), "integrate and evaluate information" (SL.CCR.2), and "evaluate a speaker's point of view, reasoning, and use of evidence" (SL.CCR.3). These are high-level thinking skills, which is why Circle of Knowledge discussions are built around serious, thought-provoking questions. Circle of Knowledge develops students' thinking through provisional writing and effective questioning techniques and has students work in small groups to integrate and evaluate ideas before participating in the larger discussion.

3. Discussions build collaborative and interpersonal skills. The introduction to the Common Core State Standards for English Language Arts and Literacy (NGA Center & CCSSO, 2010a) reminds us that the "twenty-first-century classroom and workplace are settings in which people from often widely divergent cultures and who represent diverse experiences and perspectives must learn and work together" (p. 7). To thrive in these characteristically diverse settings, students need to learn to listen attentively, appreciate opposing points of view, and disagree without "steamrolling" (or being steamrolled by) their peers. Well-designed Circle of Knowledge discussions, in which the teacher establishes communication protocols, allows students to work in both small and large groups, and gradually hands over more responsibility to students, give students the practice and support they need to build these essential interpersonal skills.

The Research Behind Circle of Knowledge

Discussion is an essential component of any thoughtful classroom. The problem is that in many classrooms, what goes by the name *discussion* is actually *recitation*—that form of discourse in which the teacher asks recall questions and gets short answers back from students. In these situations, students are rarely given time to think deeply about the content. In fact, they are rarely encouraged to think at all. Usually, three or four students dominate the conversation. Once one of these students gives the correct answer, the class moves on to the next question, and the discussion is over before it begins.

On the other hand, when classroom discussions are going well, they are nearly magical. Students come to life, ideas get taken apart and put back together, and the teacher gets a wealth of formative assessment data that reveal how well students understand key content and how deeply they are thinking about that content. What's more, research shows that students in discussion-rich classrooms experience real academic and social benefits: deeper comprehension, greater empathy and respect for their peers, and an increased ability to handle rigorous content (Polite & Adams, 1997; Tanner & Casados, 1998; Tredway, 1995).

In synthesizing the research on classroom discussion, we have identified three essential criteria for successful discussions, including

1. A high degree of student participation.

2. A strong focus on essential content.

3. High levels of thinking.

Circle of Knowledge is highly dependent on a number of techniques, or "moves," that teachers make during the discussion to meet these three criteria. We describe these moves in the following sections.

Moves for Successful Classroom Discussions

Moves for Increasing Participation

Allow students to test and share ideas in small groups. Having time to think and talk usually makes for better responses. After posing an open-ended question, let students share and compare their answers with a neighbor or in a small group. Keep the conversation focused by giving groups a specific task: "Work together to make a list of how your responses are similar and different."

Use a variety of recognition techniques. When calling on students, don't limit yourself to student volunteering, random calling, or surveying. You can significantly increase the level and quality of student participation by using these additional techniques:

- *Student calling,* in which one student addresses a question to another, encourages students to stop talking to you and start engaging with one another.

- *Round robin,* which gives every student a turn to talk, creates the expectation that students will have an opportunity and a responsibility to speak. It is especially useful for students who feel anxious about sharing.

- *Sampling,* or asking the same question to a number of students in succession, helps establish a pool or range of ideas.

- *Redirection,* redirecting a student's question to another student or to the group as a whole, gets the class to explore a student-raised proposition.

The takeaway message is variety. When you use multiple recognition techniques, you can move more easily from a question-and-answer session to genuine discussion.

Court controversy. Nothing piques interest quite like controversy. Build your discussions around truly provocative ideas and questions: Should there be a minimum age for using social networking sites? How should we remember the Age of Exploration—as a time of great discovery or one of terrible exploitation? Should intelligent design be taught in schools? Do women and men write differently?

Get students personally and actively involved. Use participation tools like Physical Barometer, People Graph, and Priority Pyramid to get all students involved and invested in the discussion.

Physical Barometer (Silver, Strong, & Perini, 2001) requires students to get up and take a physical position according to their opinions. For example, you might ask students where they stand (literally) on the issue of animal testing in scientific research: students who are opposed go to Corner A, those who support it go to Corner B, and those who are not sure stand in the middle of the room. Groups of students who hold the same position discuss their positions and then explain and defend their positions to the rest of the class. You could use Physical Barometer at both the beginning and the end of a discussion, encouraging students to reflect on how and why their positions either changed or remained the same.

People Graph is a variation on Physical Barometer. Students share their opinions about an issue or a question by lining up in the classroom or hallway along a continuum (e.g., 0–10, where 0 = strongly disagree and 10 = strongly agree) according to the strength of their opinions.

Priority Pyramid (Silver et al., 2001) asks students to rank items in order of importance using a Pyramid Organizer, with the items descending in importance from top to bottom. Students must explain the criteria they used to rank the items. For example, you might ask the class, "Which forms of renewable energy that we have discussed do you think the United States should invest in? Rank your choices from first to last, and explain the reasoning behind your ranking."

Moves for Keeping Focus

Integrate note making into discussions. Students can easily get lost if they have not pulled their thoughts together before the discussion moves on. Whenever you pose a question, or whenever students simply need time to stop and think, let them jot down some notes. You can help them focus their ideas with a Memory Box or MVP (Silver, Brunsting, & Walsh, 2008). With a Memory Box, students draw a box on a sheet of paper and are given a minute or two to fill the box with everything they can remember about a particular topic. MVP has students identify the "most valuable point" from the lesson and explain why they selected it.

Record responses and summarize frequently. Discussions comprise the contributions of many, which makes their structure hard to see. To establish and maintain focus, you need to *record, clarify,* and *summarize* participants' contributions to the discussion.

- To *record* a discussion, jot down key ideas on the board. Draw lines between statements to suggest relationships based on agreement or disagreement. Recording slows the pace of discussion and gives students more time to think. On the other hand, too much recording can hinder the excitement of a discussion. If you see this happening, wait for a natural stopping point, and then use the recording process to review the ground covered.

- To *clarify* a discussion, ask students to restate what previous speakers have said.

- To *summarize* a discussion, stop every five minutes or so and ask students to paraphrase the ideas that are on the table. If students have trouble summarizing, help them by asking a prompting question, such as "Do I hear you saying...?" After collecting several summaries, help your students combine them into a group summary.

Moves for Encouraging High Levels of Thinking

Encourage students to stop and think about the question. Impulsiveness is the enemy of deep thinking. You can help students slow down and internalize the discussion question by writing the question on the board, asking students to repeat the question to themselves, and encouraging students to imagine possible answers.

Use Q-SPACE to shape discussions. Q-SPACE (Strong et al., 1998) stands for

- **Q**uestion. Pose a question that requires thinking. Make sure all students understand what you are asking.

- **S**ilence and wait time. Remember that students need three to five seconds of wait time to process a question in adequate depth (Rowe, 1978; Stahl, 1994). Give students five seconds to find or extend their response.

- **P**robe. Help students expose and articulate their thinking with questions like "How did you come up with that idea? Can you tell me more?" Ask students to present evidence and examples to support their responses.

- **A**ccept. Accept every response, but keep the discussion going by not affirming or correcting students' responses too often. Affirmation and correction signal the end of thinking to many students.

- **C**larify. Ask students to restate their own—and other students'—ideas.

- **E**laborate. Work with students to take their ideas further. Try using a "What if?" question, or present a counterargument and ask students to respond to it. Encourage students to draw conclusions and make generalizations. Help them refine their conclusions and generalizations through further discussion.

Ask students to reflect on the quality of their contributions. Teach students what it means to be thoughtful participants in a discussion by encouraging them to monitor and reflect on their performance. To build metacognitive and reflective habits in students, create a discussion report card like the one shown in Figure 4.1. Students can review the report card before the discussion, refer to it during the discussion, and use it to assess their performance afterward.

FIGURE 4.1	Effective Discussion Report Card

Name: _____ Date: _____ Discussion Topic: _____

	Not At All	Somewhat	Considerably	Extensively
I took a position, explained it clearly, and used evidence to support my ideas.				
I willingly answered people's questions about my position, and I respectfully explained or defended my position when asked. I also asked my classmates to clarify or justify their positions when appropriate.				
I listened actively and respectfully to my classmates' positions. I also compared and contrasted their ideas with my own.				
I kept an open mind and was willing to modify my own position.				
Throughout the discussion, I summarized in my mind the things that others had said.				
I was actively involved in the conversation.				

Implementing Circle of Knowledge in the Classroom

1. Spark the discussion by posing an open-ended question that hooks students into the material.

2. Give students time to stop and think about the question. You may also want students to jot down and share responses with a partner or in a small group before opening the discussion.

3. Sharpen the focus of the discussion by posing a focusing question that highlights the central topic or theme of the discussion.

4. Have students "kindle" their responses by jotting down their initial responses and then sharing and comparing their responses in small groups.

5. Engage the whole class in the discussion. Encourage students to share their ideas, respond to prompts and questions from you or other students, refine their ideas, and evaluate the depth of their understanding.

6. During the discussion, use a variety of recognition techniques (see pp. 39–40) to maximize participation. Use Q-SPACE (see p. 42) to shape the discussion.

7. Record students' responses and summarize key content with students.

8. Allow students to reflect on the discussion and their own participation.

9. Synthesize student learning with a task that asks them to apply what they learned during the discussion.

Circle of Knowledge Sample Lessons

Sample Lesson 1: High School Geometry

Note: The following sample lesson has been adapted from The Strategic Teacher: Selecting the Right Research-Based Strategy for Every Lesson *(Silver, Strong, & Perini, 2007).*

Purpose. High school geometry teacher Eileen Cho believes that too many math classrooms run through important concepts too quickly, sealing students off from the provocative issues and ideas that make mathematics interesting. So she builds "big idea" discussions into the culture of her class-room. It is the second week of school. Students have made "multimedia" notes (notes that include verbal, visual, and mathematical information) on the key concepts in the course: *point, line, angle, line segment,* and so on. Eileen believes that students are ready for their first big idea discussion.

Sparking question. Eileen begins the discussion by posing this ques-tion: "How do you know when something is real?" Students take a few minutes to jot down some ideas in their Learning Logs and then share and compare ideas in groups of four. After small-group sharing, Eileen conducts a classwide discussion.

Eileen: OK, who has an idea? Stephan?

Stephan: Well, I think you know something is real if you can see it.

Eileen: I see a lot of hands that just went up when you said that, so I'm going to check in with someone else. Casey, what did Stephan say that provoked your reaction?

Casey: There are lots of things you can see that aren't real. Like in the mov-ies. With special effects, you can "see" dragons and spaceships . . . do you see what I'm saying, Stephan?

Stephan: Yeah, you're right. What I mean is if you can sense it, if you can see it and touch it and smell it, then it's real.

Eileen: OK, can we agree that one way we know something is real is through our senses? Good. Who has another idea? Tonia?

Tonia: Well, I agree that senses are one way to find out if something's real, but not the only way. To me, something's only real if you can feel it. Like happiness, or sadness, or love. If you can feel it in your heart, then it's real.

Eileen: That's very interesting, Tonia. Let's summarize where we are. We have two ideas: one is that "real" is confirmed by the senses. The other is that we know things are real when we can feel them. What does the class think? Which idea do you agree with more?

After a few minutes, Eileen sharpens the discussion's focus by explain-ing that many of the world's great thinkers and mathematicians have been taken up by this same question and that two of the most important minds in history—Plato and Einstein—have explored the question as it relates specifically to geometry.

Focusing question. Eileen distributes three brief readings. One is Plato's argument that geometric figures are ideal forms that exist only in the mind. Another is Einstein's explanation of how geometry is the result of human discovery. The third lays out the "mirror" argument, which claims that geometry simply reflects what we see in nature (e.g., the line of the horizon becomes the geometric line). Eileen poses a focusing question— "How does each of these three positions contribute to or conflict with your understanding of geometry?"—and gives students time to read, make notes, and prepare for the next round of discussion.

Eileen encourages student participation using a variety of recognition techniques and provides various forms of feedback depending on where she wants the discussion to go. Sometimes she requests clarification or elaboration; other times, she helps students rethink their responses. Sometimes she remains silent.

Before the discussion ends, Eileen asks students to summarize what they have learned and records their ideas on the board. Students' responses include "There is no simple agreement about where geometry is real," "Most of us had no idea this topic was up for debate," and brief summaries of each argument (e.g., "Plato claims geometric figures are ideal forms in our minds").

Synthesis activity. For homework, Eileen asks students to select the reading that most resembles their own position and defend it against the other two.

Sample Lesson 2: English Language Arts and Social Studies

Purpose. Students in Sam Carlyle's 2nd grade class are learning about the Underground Railroad. The class has just finished reading F. N. Monjo's *The Drinking Gourd*, a chapter book about a family of abolitionists who help a family of runaway slaves to freedom. At the heart of the book lies a question that is provocative for readers of any age: When is it acceptable to break the law? Sam is using Circle of Knowledge to help students explore and develop their own perspective on this rich and controversial question.

Sparking questions. Why do we have laws? What do laws do for us?

Focusing question. Were the Fullers right to break the law?

Synthesis activity. With Sam's help, students write an "I think" essay, taking a position on whether the Fullers were right or wrong to break the law.

Sample Lesson 3: Middle School Science

Purpose. As part of their unit on genetics, Carla Giordana's students are exploring the controversy related to genetically modified foods. Carla wants students to formulate and express their own opinions about this controversial topic through discussion. Before the discussion begins, students read two brief articles on genetically modified foods—one for and one against. They also use the Physical Barometer tool to group themselves according to the strength of their opinions (Strongly Oppose, Oppose, Support, Strongly Support) and engage in initial discussions in smaller opinion-based groups.

Sparking questions. What roles do values and morals play when it comes to scientific progress? Can science go too far?

Focusing questions. How can we decide whether the benefits of genetically modified food outweigh the concerns and risks surrounding it? What role should the public play in this debate? What role should the government play?

Synthesis activity. Students group themselves again using the Physical Barometer tool and explain why their positions did or did not change as a result of the discussion. Each Physical Barometer group develops a public service announcement that either warns against or touts the benefits of genetically modified food, depending on the group's position.

Planning Considerations

Good discussions take planning. To plan a Circle of Knowledge discussion, ask yourself the following questions:

- **What are my topic and my purpose?** Look for topics that are magnets for controversy, invite differing perspectives, and will engage students in deep exploration. Once you have your topic, think about your purpose. Do you want students to debate without coming to a resolution? To reach a resolution or a near-resolution? To develop a new perspective on the content? Make sure the topic and purpose align with the standards you intend to address.

- **How will my focusing question(s) set up the discussion?** Focusing questions connect the opening discussion generated by the sparking question to the actual content, thus fueling the body of the discussion. From the focusing question, the structure of the discussion will unfold. You may need only one focusing question for your discussion, or you may need two or three to lead the discussion down important paths. In all cases, focusing questions need to be broad and open-ended so that the discussion has plenty of room to grow. For example, a U.S. history teacher who wants students to explore the concept of checks and balances might ask, "Is there really a balance of power among the branches of government?"

- **How will my sparking question(s) generate student interest and activate prior knowledge?** Sparking questions come before focusing questions in the lesson sequence. Their purpose is to help students draw on their life experiences and prior knowledge for material to bring to the discussion. For example, the teacher leading a lesson on checks and balances might pose these sparking questions to open the discussion: "What First Amendment rights are especially important to you? How are all three branches of the government involved in protecting those rights?"

- **How will students acquire the necessary information?** Most Circle of Knowledge discussions require students to use and refer to information sources to help them support their ideas. You can also use information sources to introduce new content into the discussion. What information sources will students need during this discussion? Their notes? A reading? A website? A mini-lecture or demonstration from you?

- **How will I use effective discussion techniques to run the discussion?** See pages 39–43 for our discussion of moves or techniques that increase participation, keep students focused, and deepen student thinking.

- **What will students do as a result of the discussion?** How will students pull together and apply what they have learned from the discussion? You could have them mount a defense of their opinions, write a summary of the class's various ideas and opinions, create a visual organizer or map highlighting the key ideas, write a formal essay, or make a multimedia presentation.

Writing Extension: Circle of Knowledge

Many of the thinking "moves" that students need to make during a Circle of Knowledge discussion—clarifying ideas, elaborating responses, using evidence, responding to counterarguments, and so on—are the same moves that underlie good writing. Highlight these moves and connect them to the writing process by giving students writing assignments that stem from a class discussion. For example, "We've had a rich discussion on what makes art *art,* and we've looked at three different artists' definitions of art. Which definition do you most agree with? In your response, make sure you address and respond to the other two definitions."

5
Write to Learn

Write to Learn in a Nutshell

Write to Learn is a set of nested tools for writing and learning in all content areas. Careful use of the tools embedded in this strategy can drastically improve students' thinking, deepen their comprehension of content, and help teachers conduct the kind of formative assessment needed to improve student writing without getting caught in an endless cycle of paperwork. These tools support three different types of classroom writing, including

- *Provisional writing,* or brief, daily writing that supports learning.
- *Readable writing,* which requires students to clarify and organize their thinking to develop on-demand essays or responses.
- *Polished writing,* which engages students in the full writing and revision process.

Three Reasons for Using Write to Learn to Address the Common Core

1. Writing develops higher-order thinking. If we could distill the Common Core State Standards into one overarching theme, it would likely be "Develop students' higher-order and critical thinking skills." Writing "allows us to see conceptual relationships, to acquire insights, and to unravel the logic of what was previously murky or confusing" (Schmoker, 2011, p. 211). Write to Learn maximizes the benefits of writing as a "thinking builder." Provisional writing helps students get their thinking out in the open where it can be assessed and refined, while readable writing and polished writing help students shape their thinking into more powerful, refined products.

2. Writing in different text types. The Common Core's Anchor Standards for Writing have identified three types of text that are particularly important to ensuring students' readiness for college and careers in the 21st century: arguments (W.CCR.1); informative/explanatory texts (W.CCR.2); and narratives (W.CCR.3). Write to Learn helps develop students' skills in these areas by requiring students to develop high-quality written responses on demand (readable writing) and engaging students in the extended writing and revision process (polished writing). The polished writing process also includes self-assessment and peer revision—two elements integral to Writing Anchor Standard 5 (W.CCR.5).

3. Range of writing. Writing Anchor Standard 10 makes it clear that classrooms must incorporate writing "for a range of tasks, purposes, and audiences" (W.CCR.10). Write to Learn supports this level of infusion by providing teachers and students with various writing formats and tools that support a wide range of objectives and writing demands.

The Research Behind Write to Learn

How important is writing to academic success? To find out, researchers from Vanderbilt University (Graham & Hebert, 2010) conducted a meta-analysis of more than 100 studies on writing in the classroom. They found that asking students to write regularly about the texts they read in science, social studies, and language arts has a significant and positive influence on student comprehension. Douglas Reeves (2002) has similarly found that writing is "the skill most directly related to improved scores in reading, social studies, science, and even mathematics" (p. 5). Reeves also reminds us of something that too often gets lost in our concern over test scores: that writing brings "engagement, interest, and fun" (p. 5) to the classroom. Whether you are worried about raising students' test scores or worried that too much testing is getting in the way of student enjoyment, writing will make your classroom better.

Being able to write well is also an essential skill for college and career readiness, which is why the Common Core gives it so much attention. According to David Conley (2007), perhaps the foremost expert on college readiness, "If we could institute only one change to make students more college ready, it should be to increase the amount and quality of writing students are expected to produce" (pp. 27–28).

Write to Learn is a versatile strategy for increasing both the quantity and the quality of student writing in our classrooms. It provides teachers with ready-to-use tools to turn writing into a daily habit, prepare students for the kinds of writing tasks that are crucial to their academic success, and develop students' abilities to self-assess and collaborate with fellow writers to produce high-quality written work.

It also increases teachers' capacity to provide students with focused, formative feedback on their writing, a practice that improves students' writing and learning dramatically (Graham, Harris, & Hebert, 2011). The three types of writing embedded in the strategy enable teachers to assess how well students can express their understanding (provisional writing); shape their thinking and writing to respond to on-demand tasks (readable writing); and commit to making their work better through the full writing and revision process (polished writing).

Implementing Write to Learn in the Classroom

Writing is as flexible and inexhaustible as language itself, meaning that no single classroom technique or set of implementation steps can effectively capture its dynamic power. For this reason, Write to Learn involves three different kinds of writing: provisional, readable, and polished. Here, we discuss each type of writing and present a set of classroom tools that teachers can use to help students gain proficiency in all three types.

Provisional Writing

Provisional writing is a form of quick writing, like brainstorming, that slows down and opens up the thinking process. Students write spontaneously for two to five minutes to generate, clarify, or extend ideas or to react to important content. Teachers can use provisional writing in a variety of ways: to capture student interest, draw out prior knowledge, review and check understanding of content, provoke thinking, and spur reflection. Spelling and grammar are rarely assessed at the provisional level; usually, the only assessment criterion is that students actually do the writing, although sometimes teachers indicate the number of ideas or answers that students need to generate and check to see whether all students have come up with the required number.

Provisional Writing Tools

Learning Logs. A Learning Log is an active response journal that infuses writing into the daily instructional routine. Learning Logs are also ideal formative assessment tools, giving teachers real insight into what students know and how they feel about what they are learning. Here are a few tips for getting the most out of these versatile tools:

- Remind students that their Learning Logs give them the opportunity to clarify and develop their thinking without worrying about grades.

- Have students write in their Learning Logs at least once every day.

- As often as possible, have students share their responses in pairs or small groups. Encourage group members to look for similarities and differences in their responses, help one another refine and synthesize ideas, or generate additional ideas. Listen in as the groups talk.

- Connect students' written and group responses to a larger classroom discussion in which you survey students' ideas, record them on the board, and explore them further.

- Take advantage of the formative assessment opportunities that Learning Logs offer. Walk around the room as students write in their Learning Logs and as they work in groups to get a sense of their understanding. Adjust instruction according to what you learn. For example, if you find that most students cannot remember the key ingredients for photosynthesis, you probably need to reteach that content.

- Regularly comment on each student's Learning Log—once a week, if possible. Focus on a single entry and record your thoughts, questions, or feedback directly in the student's Learning Log. The best comments relate to specific ideas in the student's writing and tend to raise questions or express appreciation.

You can prompt students to write in their Learning Logs before, during, and after instructional segments to meet a variety of instructional purposes, including

- Engaging student interest in the learning to come. For example, "Why do we need pests like insects? Would we be better off if we got rid of them?"

- Activating students' prior knowledge. For example, "What comes to mind when you hear the term *statistics*?"

- Checking for understanding. For example, "What are the phases of mitosis? Briefly describe each."

- Spurring creative thinking. For example, "If you could add any feature to an amphibian to help it survive, what would you add?"

- Fostering analysis and critical thinking. For example, "How are fractions and decimals similar? How are they different?"

- Encouraging students to make personal connections to the content. For example, "Did you like the poem? Give three reasons why or why not."

- Helping students reflect on their learning. For example, "What aspects of the material are clear to you? What are you still unclear about?"

4-2-1 Free Write. This tool (Silver et al., 2001) addresses two issues that sometimes plague content-based provisional writing. First, it helps students focus their writing on the most important ideas through a process of collaborative summarization. Second, it prevents students from getting stuck when they write. 4-2-1 Free Write works like this:

1. After a reading, lecture, or other learning experience, ask students to generate the four most important ideas.

2. Have students meet in pairs to share their ideas and agree on the two most important ideas from their lists.

3. Pair up the pairs into groups of four. Each group must agree on the single most important idea. Depending on students' facility with this process, you may choose to survey students' ideas, record them on the board, and then identify (or refine) the most important idea with the class.

4. Ask all students to free-write about the big idea for three to five minutes, explaining what they know well enough that someone who has never heard of the idea could understand it. Students may not stop writing at any point during the allotted time. If they get stuck, they should write about why they are stuck. Alternately, you can have students use the 4-2-1 Summarize variation (Boutz et al., 2012), in which students use the ideas they generated during Steps 2 and 3 as supporting details in their summaries.

5. Students return to their groups, listen to one another's responses, and participate in a class discussion of the big idea.

Readable Writing

Readable writing, like a classroom essay test or assignment, requires students to clarify their thoughts and develop an organizational structure for their ideas. Unlike provisional writing, readable writing is intended for an audience—usually the teacher, who uses it to assess students' depth of understanding and ability to construct soundly reasoned responses.

Because readable writing assignments have straightforward criteria for assessment, readable writing is a great tool for developing students' skills in the key text types highlighted by Anchor Standards 1, 2, and 3 for Writing (arguments, informative/explanatory texts, and narratives) and in key writing genres addressed in the Common Core reading standards (comparison, analysis, and description). Here are some sample writing prompts that align with these text types:

- **Argument.** Based on the article we just read on the dangers of mobile phones, do you think there should be a minimum age for children to carry mobile phones? Use specific information from the article to defend your position.

- **Informative/explanatory text.** Water freezes at 32°F. Explain why it sometimes snows when the temperature is warmer than 32°F.

- **Narrative.** We have learned a lot about honeybees. Now it's your turn to imagine yourself as a honeybee. Give yourself a name, draw yourself, and describe three things you do during your day.

- **Comparison.** Our textbook includes two primary accounts of the events at Wounded Knee: one from a member of the Lakota tribe and one from a U.S. soldier. Compare these eyewitness accounts. In your essay, make sure you address these two questions: What is the tone of each written account? What does the tone reveal about the author's perspective of the events?

- **Analysis (textual).** Select one of Edgar Allan Poe's horror stories that we read during this unit. Conduct a literary analysis of the story by explaining how Poe achieves the "unity of effect" he describes in his essay "The Philosophy of Composition."

- **Analysis (mathematical).** Analyze the data charts showing the sales for best-selling fiction titles in hardcover, paperback, and e-book formats over the last 10 years. What conclusions can you draw? What do you anticipate the sales in each format to be 10 years from now? Explain your reasoning.

- **Description.** After reading the first few vignettes in Sandra Cisneros's *The House on Mango Street*, briefly describe the character Esperanza and her Chicago neighborhood.

You should assign readable writing tasks regularly, both to help students improve their ability to construct quality written responses and to build up a bank of material for formative and summative assessment. Keep in mind that you do not have to grade all readable writing. If during the course of the year you assign 12 readable writing tasks, grading 4 of them will give you plenty of assessment data to track students' evolution as writers. Meanwhile, the other pieces will give you and your students lots of good formative assessment data on their mastery of the content and their thinking and writing skills.

When you evaluate readable writing, it's less important to assess mechanics like grammar and spelling than it is to ascertain the accuracy and organization of main ideas and supporting details and the quality of student thinking. Remember, this is called "readable writing" for a reason: it should make sense and be easy to understand. As a side note, all readable writing should be double-spaced. Double-spaced writing takes less time to read and provides space for teachers to jot down comments and students to make edits.

Readable Writing Tools

3 x 3 Writing Frame. Some students struggle with on-demand writing tasks because they have a hard time seeing the overall structure of the writing they are being asked to produce. As a result, their writing lacks focus, moving from one idea to the next without a sense of how the parts fit together to form a whole. The 3 x 3 Writing Frame uses a simple visual organizer to help students see the structure of a good essay and plan out its beginning, middle, and end. The frame can be easily adapted to fit the three text types highlighted in the Common Core: argument (W.CCR.1), informative/explanatory (W.CCR.2), and narrative (W.CCR.3). Figure 5.1 (pp. 58–59) shows sample frames completed by an elementary school student for a persuasive essay and a middle school student for a personal narrative.

Building Writing. Building Writing (Boutz et al., 2012) is a prewriting tool that provides the scaffolding emerging writers need as they learn to produce high-quality responses on demand. The tool builds students' motivation and confidence as writers, allowing them to earn advance points toward their final writing grade and leaving them with an outline that they can use to guide their writing. It also permits teachers to formatively assess every student's work in nearly real time. Here's how it works:

1. Pose a question that tests students' understanding of key content (for example, "Why do we breathe?"). Give students five minutes to brainstorm their initial ideas. You may pose the question days before the actual writing activity to give students time to think and collect notes.

2. Walk around the room to review students' responses and let them know how many points they have earned so far. In a typical Building Writing assignment, you would reward students 5 points for each idea that addresses the question, for a possible total of 15 points. For the question "Why do we breathe?" a student might get the full 15 points for generating these three ideas: (1) Breathing is how the body gets oxygen; (2) Oxygen is needed to create energy; (3) Breathing releases waste as carbon dioxide.

3. Ask students to pair up. Student pairs can earn up to 10 points by elaborating on their initial ideas, revising them, generating new ones, or providing appropriate supporting details.

FIGURE 5.1   Sample 3 x 3 Writing Frames

Elementary School: Persuasive Frame

Beginning What are you trying to prove?	Middle What is your evidence? Prove it.		End Close the writing.
Make your case or restate the question.	*Magic THREES: Reasons, Causes, Purposes*	*Elaborate on each reason (or provide an example).*	*Wrap it up.*
Harriet Tubman is a person to be admired, even today.	• One reason: Brave • Another reason: Smart • Finally: Not selfish	• Risked her life to free people from slavery. • Helped create the Underground Railroad. • Sacrificed her own life to make sure her children and grandchildren would never be slaves.	Harriet Tubman saved many people from a life of slavery. She should be remembered for her courage.

Middle School: Personal Narrative Frame

Beginning What personal story are you telling?	Middle What are the key developments in your story?		End Close the writing.
What message/idea do you want to convey?	*Magic THREES: Identify three key points in the story.*	*Make each point come to life with details, sensory language, and dialogue.*	*Go for an ending that clarifies your message and gets noticed.*
I'll tell about the time I went to the haunted house down the shore. I want to show how I overcame my fear and learned to love haunted houses.	1. When we first got there, I was terrified.	• Blood-curdling screams were coming from inside. My heart was beating like a drumroll. I've never sweated so much, not even during my basketball games.	I want my ending to clarify my message that fear can be overcome. I know because it happened to me.

FIGURE 5.1	Sample 3 x 3 Writing Frames (continued)

Middle School: Personal Narrative Frame (continued)

Beginning What personal story are you telling?	Middle What are the key developments in your story?		End Close the writing.
What message/idea do you want to convey?	*Magic THREES: Identify three key points in the story.*	*Make each point come to life with details, sensory language, and dialogue.*	*Go for an ending that clarifies your message and gets noticed.*
Catchy opening: "It all happened one spooky October night."	2. Inside the haunted house, people and things were jumping out at us. 3. Once it was over, I realized how much fun I had had.	• A giant spider fell from the ceiling. I screamed when a man with a chainsaw jumped out at us. • I was laughing so hard I couldn't stop. Joe and I started comparing our favorite parts. We decided to go again.	I think a great last sentence would be: "Now, as soon as there is that October chill in the air, I look forward to a good old-fashioned scare at the Sandy Point haunted house."

4. Allow students to share their ideas with the class. Lead the discussion and record ideas as needed to ensure that all students have a strong grasp of the key ideas and details before they begin writing. Ask students to assess their performance during the discussion by awarding themselves up to 10 points based on how well they shared ideas; listened to others; questioned, added to, or summarized others' ideas; and used the discussion to refine their list of ideas.

5. Challenge students to write a topic sentence and organize their ideas into a simple outline. Award up to 5 points for the topic sentence (Does it address the question and set up the paragraph? Is it clear?) and up to 10 points for the outline (Is the information organized logically?). For example, a student might write

Breathing has two major functions. (5 points)

First, it brings oxygen into the body:

- Inhaling allows oxygen to enter the body through the lungs.
- Oxygen dissolves in blood, is carried to cells, and is used to create energy.

10 points for organized outline

Second, it eliminates waste:

- Blood carries waste back to the lungs.
- Exhaling releases carbon dioxide.

6. Have students draft their responses. Before students begin writing, clarify the criteria you will use to assess their written responses. You may want to provide a checklist or rubric to help guide students' writing.

7. Award students up to 50 points for their drafts. Add these points to their existing points to get a total score. Using the assessment criteria to guide you, provide students with usable feedback on their work.

Polished Writing

Polished writing engages students in the full writing process, from coming up with initial ideas to writing a final draft. The process moves through a set of progressive phases. First, students give an overall shape to their ideas by generating notes, organizers, outlines, or any combination of the three. Next, students produce a first draft (writing on every other line, as with readable writing) and read it against a set of specific criteria, which they use to revise their pieces. After correcting their first drafts, students create second drafts, which they read aloud to an audience. The audience provides a last round of feedback that students use to create their final drafts.

Polished Writing Tools

Writing folders. Writing folders structure the complex processes associated with polished writing. The folders house students' ongoing work—the records and artifacts of the writing process. Students can make their own writing folders by folding one piece of 12" x 18" construction paper in half lengthwise, placing a second piece of 12" x 18" paper (preferably of another color) into the crease of the first, and then folding both pieces widthwise. Taping each side to make pockets creates a four-pocket folder. Each pocket corresponds to one of the four phases in producing polished writing.

Pocket 1: Initial ideas. Students keep their prewriting and planning documents, such as organizers, notecards, and outlines, in this pocket.

Pocket 2: First draft. Students correct and revise their first drafts by reading them against a set of criteria, such as the following:

- Is the content accurate?
- Are all the big ideas and key details included?
- Does your draft have a clear beginning, middle, and end?
- Do you predict and respond to possible counterarguments?
- Do you use vivid examples to support your argument and make your writing memorable?
- Does your work contain a mix of different sentence types?
- Does your piece include relevant academic vocabulary?

Pocket 3: Second draft. Students use the third pocket to shape their first draft into a second draft. Students read aloud their second drafts to a group of fellow writers called a Writer's Club. After the reading, members of the Writer's Club provide feedback and constructive criticism based on three criteria:

- Does the composition complete the requirements of the assignment?
- Does it sound good? Is it highly readable?
- Has the writer used the specific first-draft criteria to check and revise the composition?

Pocket 4: Final draft. The fourth pocket houses the final draft. In developing their final drafts, students make adjustments according to the feedback they received from their Writer's Clubs. Students also use this pocket to reflect on their work and the process they went through to create and refine it. You can encourage students' reflective writing by providing them with prompts like these:

- What do you like most about your composition?
- How do you believe you have improved as a writer?
- What new insights into the writing process have you discovered?

Writer's Club. Feedback from peers helps writers weed out weaknesses and fine-tune their craft. The Writer's Club is a support and feedback group for writers that can be set up in various ways. For example, members can choose to read their own pieces aloud, or members can read one another's pieces to help each writer notice where his or her writing causes the reader to falter. The following steps (Boutz et al., 2012) outline a powerful way to use Writer's Clubs in the classroom:

1. Organize students into Writer's Clubs with three to five members.

2. Have students read their pieces aloud and request feedback from their peers. The nature of the feedback can be determined by you or by students. Options include

    - Telling students which criteria to focus on. For example, "When listening to one another's stories, keep these questions in mind: Does it have a clear beginning, middle, and end? Did it capture your interest? Did the writer use the suspense techniques we've discussed?"

    - Allowing students to request particular kinds of feedback from their classmates. For example, "My closing doesn't have as strong an effect as I'd like. Does anyone have any suggestions?"

    - Distributing the Writer's Club discussion questions (see Figure 5.2, p. 64) and letting students choose which ones to respond to. Modify the list as needed for specific types of writing tasks or for use with younger students.

3. Encourage students to listen carefully and be ready to share their thoughts. Remind them that effective feedback is

    - Specific. (What exactly did the writer do well?)

    - Improvement-oriented. (What can the writer do to make his or her work better?)

    - About the work, not the student. (Say "Your thesis was original," not "You're a good writer.")

4. Have students synthesize the feedback they receive and use it to revise and refine their drafts. You may also want club members to meet again to review and discuss their revisions.

Figure 5.2 shows sample Writer's Club discussion questions.

Planning Considerations

As you plan for the regular use of writing activities and assessments in your classroom, consider the following questions:

- In this particular lesson, what is your purpose in having students write? Do you want your students to generate ideas, analyze, synthesize, judge, recall, anticipate, define? What standards do you intend to address?

- Will students' responses be used as part of the ongoing process of learning (provisional writing)? Or will the writing be more like a classroom assignment designed to prepare students for on-demand writing tasks (readable writing)? Or will the writing lead to a comprehensive and refined product (polished writing)?

- How can you best phrase your writing prompt to elicit responses that will be useful in achieving your purpose?

- When is the best time in the learning sequence for students to respond to the prompt?

- What should the final responses look and sound like? Will you need to develop a rubric or checklist to help your students understand your expectations?

- Will you need to build in time for students to reflect on and rethink what they have originally written? One simple but powerful technique that can help with post-writing reflection is What? So What? Now What? (Silver et al., 2001). To use this technique, ask students to answer

  — **What?** What did you do during this process?
  — **So what?** What did you learn about yourself, the content, or the writing process?
  — **Now what?** How can you use or apply what you have learned?

FIGURE 5.2 Writer's Club Discussion Questions

Rules of the Writer's Club
1. Everyone reads.
2. Writers choose one or more questions for listeners to respond to.
3. Listeners give additional feedback by choosing other questions to answer.
4. Writers listen to responses without becoming defensive.
5. Writers use what they learn to revise and improve their work.

Follow the guidelines for productive discussions at all times:
Take turns talking, ask and answer questions, listen respectfully to others' ideas, and build on what others have to say.

Literal Questions	Personal Perspective Questions
• What is this piece about? What are the key points? • How would you summarize this piece? • Does the piece address the question? • Are any important ideas or details missing? • Are there any factual or grammatical errors that should be fixed?	• How did this piece make you feel? • If this were your piece, what aspect of it would you be most proud of? • Did you learn anything from this piece that could help you as a writer? • Who is the intended audience? Did the writer address the needs and interests of the intended audience?
Analytical Questions	**Original Thinking Questions**

• What are the greatest strengths of this piece? What could be improved?
• How well did the writer fulfill the requirements of this text type?
  – Argument (W.CCR.1): How clear and well supported is the writer's position?
  – Informative/explanatory text (W.CCR.2): How clearly and accurately is the topic explained?
  – Narrative (W.CCR.3): How clearly and vividly described is the event/experience?
• How does this piece compare with other pieces this writer has composed?
	• If this piece were a type of clothing, music, or weather, what would it be, and why?
	• What might be the effect of adding or deleting _____ from the piece?
	• What are some possible ways to improve this piece?
	• Did the writer "paint a picture" with words? Were you able to see the ideas and images in your mind?

Source: Adapted from *Tools for Thoughtful Assessment*, by A. L. Boutz, H. F. Silver, J. W. Jackson, and M. J. Perini, 2012, Ho-Ho-Kus, NJ: Thoughtful Education Press. © 2012 Silver Strong & Associates/Thoughtful Education Press. Used with permission.

6
Vocabulary's CODE

Vocabulary's CODE in a Nutshell

Vocabulary's CODE is a strategic approach to direct vocabulary instruction that helps students master crucial concepts and retain new vocabulary terms. Students work their way from initial exposure to in-depth understanding through a series of progressive learning activities, which help students "crack" Vocabulary's CODE. This learning series entails

- Connecting with new words.
- Organizing new words into meaningful categories.
- Deep-processing the most important concepts and terms.
- Exercising the mind through strategic review and practice.

Three Reasons for Using Vocabulary's CODE to Address the Common Core

1. Vocabulary is a foundation for improved literacy. Three of the six Common Core Anchor Standards for Language are vocabulary standards (L.CCR.4, L.CCR.5, and L.CCR.6). Vocabulary is a foundational skill, and investing in vocabulary instruction pays off in all areas of literacy.

2. Academic vocabulary is at the core of the Core. The Common Core gives special attention to two types of vocabulary terms: "general academic" and "domain-specific" words and phrases (L.CCR.6). John Kendall (2011), author of *Understanding Common Core State Standards*, explains,

"General academic words, sometimes called Tier 2 words, are words that are commonly used in academic or professional writing but rarely used in speech or informal settings. Domain-specific words, sometimes called Tier 3 words, are specific to a discipline or field of study" (p. 19). These academic and domain-specific words are the words that experts use in their fields to make communication precise and powerful—and the words that students are expected to understand and use to meet Common Core State Standards for Reading, Writing, and Speaking and Listening. These academic terms are far less likely to be encountered by students through wide reading and thus need to be taught through direct vocabulary instruction.

3. Vocabulary fuels learning. As a rule, the more expansive our vocabularies are, the more background knowledge we possess. And as Robert Marzano (2004) has demonstrated, the more background knowledge we possess, the more we can learn. Direct vocabulary instruction not only increases students' ability to comprehend and retain what we are teaching today but also prepares students to be better learners in the future.

The Research Behind Vocabulary's CODE

Not so long ago, the idea that teachers should spend time teaching vocabulary was controversial. Everyone agreed that vocabulary was important: study after study shows that a rich vocabulary correlates with higher achievement, increased earning potential, and greater academic and economic opportunities. The controversy lay in what teachers were supposed to do about vocabulary. Some experts questioned the wisdom of a direct approach, arguing that there were far too many words to teach directly and that promoting wide reading was all teachers could do to build students' vocabulary.

We now know that direct vocabulary instruction is one of the single best instructional decisions a teacher can make. In *Building Background Knowledge for Academic Achievement*, Marzano (2004) shows that direct vocabulary instruction focused on essential academic terms leads to an average improvement of 33 percentile points on subject-area tests.

To realize these kinds of results, teachers need to develop an approach to vocabulary instruction that takes into account key findings from the research, such as the following:

- Vocabulary instruction has the greatest effect when it focuses on a reasonable number of important academic terms rather than on high-frequency word lists (Marzano, 2004).

- Developing anything more than a superficial understanding of new terms requires multiple exposures to the terms (Jenkins, Stein, & Wysocki, 1984).

- Understanding and retention improve when students interact with words in a variety of ways (Beck, McKeown, & Kucan, 2002).

- Students need opportunities to think deeply about new words using thinking strategies like comparison, metaphors, and nonlinguistic representation (Marzano, 2004).

Implementing Vocabulary's CODE in the Classroom

Vocabulary's CODE provides teachers with a framework and a set of instructional tools to build a four-phase learning sequence that deepens students' understanding of key words:

1. **Connect.** Because a significant number of unfamiliar terms can be daunting to students, the first phase focuses on helping students form a strong initial connection with these terms.

2. **Organize.** Students remember information better when it is clearly organized. The second phase ensures that students understand how the terms relate to one another and fit together to make up a larger structure.

3. **Deep-Process.** In the third phase, students use thinking strategies and multiple forms of representation to develop a deep, conceptual understanding of the most important vocabulary terms.

4. **Exercise.** Vocabulary terms are like muscles: skip the workouts and you'll lose the definition (pun intended). The fourth phase of Vocabulary's CODE engages students in meaningful review and practice activities that help them commit new terms to their long-term memory.

Although these four phases naturally lead students to deep understanding, the question remains of which strategies and tools to use for each phase. Figure 6.1 shows a matrix of vocabulary tools and strategies organized according to the four phases of Vocabulary's CODE. When planning your unit or learning sequence, refer to this matrix to help you select appropriate tools and ensure deep learning.

FIGURE 6.1 Matrix of Vocabulary's CODE Tools

C	O	D	E
Word Wall A collection of words is organized into categories and posted on the wall for students to use in their reading and writing.	**Prioritizing Vocabulary** The teacher or students determine which words are *essential,* which are *important,* and which are *good to know*.	**Visualizing Vocabulary** Students create images, sketches, or icons with brief explanations to demonstrate understanding.	**Vocabulary Games** Students play games like Bingo, Jeopardy!, and Word Baseball to review vocabulary in a competitive and fun manner.
Power Decoding Students use "attack skills" (prefixes, suffixes, roots, context clues, and substitutions) to decode new words.	**Concept Maps** Students create visual representations of hierarchical relationships among a central concept, supporting ideas, and important details.	**Storytelling** Students analyze a selection of stories and then use basic story elements to define important concepts.	**Use It or Lose It** Students use a specified number of new words in their writing assignments.
Associations Students generate words, pictures, feelings, physical reactions to words, or whatever else comes to mind.	**Fist Lists and Word Spiders** The teacher provides a category in the "palm" of a hand organizer, and students generate five words that fit the category, one for each "finger" of the organizer. Word Spiders are similar, only with a "body" and eight "legs."	**Metaphors and Similes** Students use words deeply by exploring their relationships to other words and concepts (e.g., How is democracy like baseball?).	**Vocabulary Carousel** The teacher sets up five or six stations that include a variety of vocabulary activities. Students rotate through all the stations, working in small groups.

Source: Adapted from *Word Works: Cracking Vocabulary's CODE* (pp. 4–5), by H. F. Silver, R. W. Strong, and M. J. Perini (Eds.), 2005, Ho-Ho-Kus, NJ: Thoughtful Education Press. © 2005 Silver Strong & Associates/Thoughtful Education Press. Used with permission.

FIGURE 6.1 Matrix of Vocabulary's CODE Tools *(continued)*

C	O	D	E
See It, Say It, Show It, Store It Students look at the word, pronounce it slowly, write it out, and record its definition in their own words.	**Word Banks** Students examine a list of words and place them into specific categories or the appropriate slots of a visual organizer.	**Defining Characteristics** Students build multilayered definitions by focusing on essential characteristics: What is it? What is it used for? Why is it valued? Where does it come from?	**Practice Makes Perfect** The teacher instructs students in the principles of effective practice, including how to mass and distribute review sessions, use words often, and make stronger connections.
Glossary Students keep a glossary of new words, defining the terms in their own words and including icons or images of the terms.	**Group and Label** Students examine a list of vocabulary words and place them into groups based on common characteristics. For each group, students devise a label that describes what all the grouped words have in common.	**Etymologies** Students investigate word histories, analyzing how a word's original meaning is intact and how it has changed.	**Three's a Crowd** Students decide which word from a group of three doesn't belong and explain why.
Word Catcher Students "catch" a new word each day and record it in their vocabulary journals.	**A Diagram to Die For** Students create a diagram that shows the relationship among the words on a Word Wall.	**Three-Way Tie** Students select three words from a unit's vocabulary and arrange them on a triangle. They connect the words with lines and explain the relationship between each pair of words by writing along the connecting lines. They may also summarize these relationships in the middle of the triangle.	**Peer Practice** Students work as peer partners. One student serves as a coach, the other as a player. While the player works to define key terms from the unit, the coach provides assistance, feedback, and praise. Students then reverse roles.

Vocabulary's CODE Sample Units

The examples that follow highlight how teachers select essential vocabulary for a unit and then use a variety of tools to move students through the four phases of Vocabulary's CODE.

Sample Vocabulary Unit 1: High School Science

Note: The following sample unit has been adapted from The Ten Attributes of Successful Learners: Mastering the Tools of Learning *(Silver, Perini, & Gilbert, 2008).*

Mirabella Santana is starting a unit on the human nervous system. She surveys her textbook to generate a list of essential vocabulary terms:

auricle	external ear	peripheral nervous
central nervous	ganglia	system (PNS)
system (CNS)	inner ear	receptors
cerebellum	medulla	response
cerebrum	middle ear	retina
choroid	neuron	sclera
cornea	olfactory epithelium	stimuli
equilibrium	olfactory nerve	subcutaneous tissue
external auditory	optic nerve	tactile corpuscles
canal	ossicles	tympanic membrane

Phase One: How will students CONNECT with the new terms? Mirabella starts off her unit by having each student complete a Vocabulary Knowledge Rating (VKR). Students rate their understanding on a 1–4 scale for each term, with 1 meaning that they have never heard of the term and 4 meaning that they know and can explain the term. Mirabella uses VKR to collect baseline data on student understanding and to help students familiarize themselves with the new terms and concepts.

Phase Two: How will students ORGANIZE the new words? Mirabella asks students to work in groups to create their own vocabulary maps. To create their maps, students look up unfamiliar words and use their textbooks to help them organize the terms in a meaningful way. Figure 6.2

shows an example of how one student group used the headings from their textbook sections to help them organize the terms.

Notice that the students incorporated some terms they already knew into their map (e.g., *spinal cord, brain, nerves*) to help them form a stronger connection to the new terms.

| FIGURE 6.2 | Nervous System Vocabulary Map |

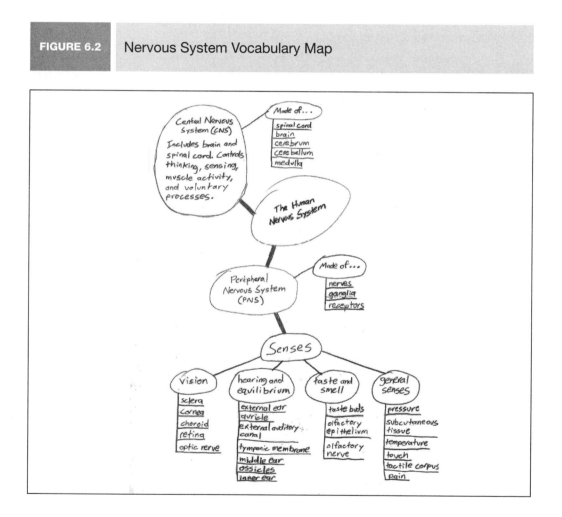

Phase Three: How will students DEEP-PROCESS the words? Over the course of the unit, students create a set of Knowledge Cards for the terms. On one side of each card is an icon or picture; on the reverse is the term followed by a brief definition. Students use their knowledge cards to quiz themselves and one another.

Phase Four: How will students EXERCISE their understanding of new words? As the unit draws to a close, Mirabella has her students complete another Vocabulary Knowledge Rating (VKR). Completing a VKR near the end of the unit helps students see how their understanding has grown. It is also a great way to help students identify terms and concepts that need more review prior to the test.

Mirabella also wants her students to demonstrate their understanding in a more substantial way—through writing. She has students summarize what they have learned with a brief para-writing activity in which they explain how the human nervous system works, incorporating as many vocabulary words as they can.

Sample Vocabulary Unit 2: Primary Mathematics

Adam Zuckerman is working with his kindergarten students to identify and analyze basic shapes. He draws this list of key vocabulary terms from the Common Core (K.G.1–3 cluster): *square*, *rectangle*, *triangle*, *hexagon*, *circle*, *cube*, *cylinder*, *cone*, and *sphere*.

Phase One: How will students CONNECT with the new terms? Adam posts each vocabulary word and its corresponding shape on a Word Wall. On the left side of the Word Wall are the two-dimensional shapes; on the right side are the three-dimensional shapes. With the Word Wall serving as a constant reminder, Adam introduces each shape one by one using the See It, Say It, Spell It, Show It technique: students see each shape on the interactive whiteboard, say each word aloud as a class, and spell each word in their "shape books" with Adam's help. Students then show each shape by tracing two-dimensional shapes and pasting images of three-dimensional shapes in their shape books.

Phase Two: How will students ORGANIZE the new words? Adam adds two new terms to the Word Wall to introduce the concepts of two-dimensional and three-dimensional figures: *flat shapes* and *solid shapes*. Because he has already posted the words and shapes in two columns, Adam writes each new term at the top of its appropriate column. He asks students to see if they can figure out why he has chosen these words to describe each set of shapes.

Phase Three: How will students DEEP-PROCESS the words? As Adam teaches students about the basic attributes of each shape, he uses a variety of processing activities to help students deepen their understanding. He has his students become

- *Shape searchers.* Students cut out pictures of each shape from magazines or printed webpages to include in their shape books.
- *Shape makers.* Students draw each "flat" shape and use manipulatives or clay to form each "solid" shape.
- *Super shape sorters.* Students pick two shapes out of a box, name each shape, and explain how they are alike and different.

Phase Four: How will students EXERCISE their understanding of new words? Adam covers up the Word Wall and provides students with two sets of cards: one set with the names of each shape and one set with the images of each shape. Students must use what they have learned to re-create the Word Wall, putting all the names and shapes in their correct categories (flat versus solid).

Sample Vocabulary Unit 3: Upper-Elementary Social Studies

Note: The following sample lesson has been adapted from Word Works: Cracking Vocabulary's CODE *(2nd ed.) (Silver, Strong, & Perini, 2008).*

Pat Schwartz is starting a unit on Ancient Egypt with her 5th graders titled "Why Is Egypt Considered the First Great Civilization?" In addition to this primary question, Pat develops four essential questions that will guide the unit. She uses these questions to organize the unit's key vocabulary terms on a Word Wall:

- What did Ancient Egyptians believe? (*polytheism, mummification, afterlife*)
- How did the Nile River help develop Ancient Egyptian culture? (*irrigation, desert, delta, fertile, river valley*)
- What was so great about Ancient Egypt? (*papyrus, hieroglyphics, scribe, Sphinx, pyramids, astronomy, surgery*)
- How was Ancient Egypt governed? (*kingdom, pharaoh, priests, Hatshepsut, Akhenaten*)

Phase One: How will students CONNECT with the new terms? To begin her unit, Pat organizes students into small cooperative teams. She gives each team an envelope containing 20 images (photographs, maps, drawings, and paintings) related to Ancient Egyptian civilization. Teams study the images and look for patterns that will help them make predictions about the unit. After each team finishes reviewing the images and making initial connections, Pat helps students create a glossary of the vocabulary words for the unit. The class defines the words and connects each one to one of the images.

Phase Two: How will students ORGANIZE the new words? Because Pat's Word Wall is organized by essential questions, it constantly reminds students of the relationships among important vocabulary words. To help students find new relationships, Pat has the class create word webs connecting key vocabulary.

Phase Three: How will students DEEP-PROCESS the words? Pat uses comparison and discussion to deepen her students' understanding of essential words and concepts. For example, she has students compare and contrast two of Ancient Egypt's most important pharaohs—Hatshepsut and Akhenaten—according to key criteria. Pat also has students rank the contributions of Ancient Egypt in order of importance as a prompt for a whole-class discussion.

Phase Four: How will students EXERCISE their understanding of new words? Near the end of the unit, Pat asks students to create a hieroglyphic for each of the words they learned and explored during the unit. Students then use their words and hieroglyphics to compose a summary that demonstrates their understanding of Ancient Egyptian civilization.

Planning Considerations

To plan a Vocabulary's CODE unit or lesson sequence, ask yourself two main questions:

What are the essential terms students need to learn? We cannot teach every word students need to know, so prioritizing terms is important. By adapting Wiggins and McTighe's (2005) model for establishing curricular priorities, you can organize unit vocabulary terms into three levels:

- *Nice-to-know words* are nouns, verbs, adjectives, adverbs, and specialized words that enrich language but are not central to understanding core content. For example, if you are teaching upper-elementary students about plants, *simple leaf* and *compound leaf* might be nice-to-know words.

- *Important words* are concepts, events, ideas, and people that deepen understanding and help students make connections to other ideas in the unit. For example, *carbon dioxide* and *chlorophyll* are important plant words.

- *Core-content words* are central concepts that serve as the foundation for the unit. *Photosynthesis* is a core-content word related to plants.

Once you have prioritized your words, it is time to create the unit's list of vocabulary terms. We recommend that you select no more than 30 words for a secondary-level unit, no more than 20 words for an elementary-level unit, and no more than 10 words for a primary-level unit.

How will I move students through the phases of CODE? Look closely at your words. Then look at the sample units (pp. 70–74) and the Vocabulary's CODE Matrix (pp. 68–69). What do you want to happen during each phase of Vocabulary's CODE? What kinds of tools from the Vocabulary's CODE Matrix will help you meet these goals? How will you use these tools to conduct formative assessment of students' growing understanding?

Writing Extension: Vocabulary's CODE

When it comes to mastering vocabulary terms, there is no substitute for use. Almost any writing assignment is an opportunity for students to use new vocabulary terms in a meaningful way. Improve students' mastery of new terms and their power as writers by requiring them to use an appropriate number of vocabulary terms in their writing assignments. For example, "Today, you'll be using what you've learned about butterflies to make a picture book. In your picture book, you'll 'be' a butterfly, and you'll tell the reader about each stage of your life. In your picture book, you must use all seven vocabulary terms on our Word Wall."

Conclusion:
Good for Teachers, Good for
Students, Good for Schools

Instructional strategies like the Core Six give teachers proven and practical ways to respond to the rigorous demands of the Common Core. When used well, they also incite students' thinking, turn the process of learning into an active quest, and build the skills students need to be ready for college and careers.

The Core Six also increase schools' capacity as professional learning communities. In high-functioning professional learning communities, educators learn together, share their best ideas with one another, and help every member improve. All of these collaborative learning activities are predicated on a common language. The Core Six are a foundation for that common language. When teachers learn a manageable number of strategies, and when these strategies are commonly named and defined, teachers can have substantive conversations just by comparing notes. From there, the conversation grows and takes on nuance: *What happened when you used Reading for Meaning with a primary document? With a word problem? With a website? How did students respond? Let's look at some of the student work we got when we used this strategy. How did the strategy help students meet Common Core State Standards? What do students still seem to be struggling with? How can we get better results next time?*

Obviously, six strategies cannot do all the heavy lifting that goes into creating a culture of professional learning. Nor do they provide teachers with everything they need to address the Common Core. But the Common Core requires a clear and committed response from teachers and their schools, and the Core Six will make that response stronger.

References

Beck, I. L., McKeown, M. G., & Kucan, L. (2002). *Bringing words to life: Robust vocabulary instruction*. New York: The Guilford Press.

Boutz, A. L., Silver, H. F., Jackson, J. W., & Perini, M. J. (2012). *Tools for thoughtful assessment*. Ho-Ho-Kus, NJ: Thoughtful Education Press.

Brown, R., Pressley, M., Van Meter, P., & Schuder, T. (1996). A quasi-experimental validation of transactional strategies instruction with low-achieving second-grade readers. *Journal of Educational Psychology, 88*(1), 18–37.

Conley, D. T. (2007). The challenge of college readiness. *Educational Leadership, 64*(7), 23–29.

Dean, C. B., Hubbell, E. R., Pitler, H., & Stone, B. (2012). *Classroom instruction that works: Research-based strategies for increasing student achievement* (2nd ed.). Alexandria, VA: ASCD.

Durkin, D. (1978/1979). What classroom observations reveal about reading comprehension instruction. *Reading Research Quarterly, 14*, 481–533.

Fredricks, J. A., Blumenfeld, P. C., & Paris, A. H. (2004). School engagement: Potential of the concept, state of the evidence. *Review of Educational Research, 74*, 59–109.

Graham, S., Harris, K., & Hebert, M. (2011). *Informing writing: The benefits of formative assessment (A report from Carnegie Corporation of New York)*. Washington, DC: Alliance for Excellent Education.

Graham, S., & Hebert, M. (2010). *Writing to read: Evidence for how writing can improve reading (A report from Carnegie Corporation of New York)*. Washington, DC: Alliance for Excellent Education.

Jenkins, J. R., Stein, M. L., & Wysocki, K. (1984). Learning vocabulary through reading. *American Educational Research Journal, 21*, 767–787.

Keene, E. O. (2010). New horizons in comprehension. *Educational Leadership, 67*(6), 69–73.

Keene, E. O., & Zimmerman, S. (2007). *Mosaic of thought: The power of comprehension strategy instruction* (2nd ed.). Portsmouth, NH: Heinemann.

Kendall, J. (2011). *Understanding common core state standards*. Alexandria, VA: ASCD.

Marzano, R. J. (2004). *Building background knowledge for academic achievement: Research on what works in schools*. Alexandria, VA: ASCD.

Marzano, R. J. (2007). *The art and science of teaching: A comprehensive framework for effective instruction*. Alexandria, VA: ASCD.

Marzano, R. J. (2010). Teaching inference. *Educational Leadership, 67*(7), 80–81.

Marzano, R. J., Pickering, D., & Pollock, J. (2001). *Classroom instruction that works: Research-based strategies for increasing student achievement*. Alexandria, VA: ASCD.

National Governors Association Center for Best Practices (NGA Center), Council of Chief State School Officers (CCSSO). (2010a). *Common core state standards for English language arts & literacy in history/social studies, science, and technical subjects*. Washington, DC: Author.

National Governors Association Center for Best Practices (NGA Center), Council of Chief State School Officers (CCSSO). (2010b). *Common core state standards for mathematics*. Washington, DC: Author.

Polite, V. C., & Adams, A. H. (1997). Critical thinking and values clarification through Socratic seminars. *Urban Education, 32*(2), 256–278.

Pressley, M. (2006). *Reading instruction that works: The case for balanced teaching* (3rd ed.). New York: The Guilford Press.

Pressley, M., & Afflerbach, P. (1995). *Verbal protocols of reading: The nature of constructively responsive reading*. Hillsdale, NJ: Lawrence Erlbaum.

Reeves, D. B. (2002). *Reason to write: Help your child succeed in school and in life through better reasoning and clear communication*. New York: Kaplan.

Rowe, M. B. (1978). Wait, wait, wait.... *School Science and Mathematics, 78*(3), 207–216.

Schmoker, M. (2011). *Focus: Elevating the essentials to radically improve student learning*. Alexandria, VA: ASCD.

Silver, H. F. (2010). *Compare & contrast: Teaching comparative thinking to strengthen student learning (A Strategic Teacher PLC Guide)*. Alexandria, VA: ASCD.

Silver, H. F., Brunsting, J. R., & Walsh, T. (2008). *Math tools, grades 3–12: 64 ways to differentiate instruction and increase student engagement*. Thousand Oaks, CA: Corwin.

Silver, H. F., Morris, S., & Klein, V. (2010). *Reading for meaning: How to build students' comprehension, reasoning, and problem-solving skills (A Strategic Teacher PLC Guide)*. Alexandria, VA: ASCD.

Silver, H. F., Perini, M. J., & Gilbert, J. M. (2008). *The ten attributes of successful learners: Mastering the tools of learning*. Ho-Ho-Kus, NJ: Thoughtful Education Press.

Silver, H. F., Strong, R. W., & Perini, M. J. (2001). *Tools for promoting active, in-depth learning*. Ho-Ho-Kus, NJ: Thoughtful Education Press.

Silver, H. F., Strong, R. W., & Perini, M. J. (Eds.). (2005). *Word works: Cracking Vocabulary's CODE (Professional Learning Portfolio)*. Ho-Ho-Kus, NJ: Thoughtful Education Press.

Silver, H. F., Strong, R. W., & Perini, M. J. (2007). *The strategic teacher: Selecting the right research-based strategy for every lesson*. Alexandria, VA: ASCD.

Silver, H. F., Strong, R. W., & Perini, M. J. (2008). *Word works: Cracking vocabulary's CODE (Professional Learning Portfolio)* (2nd ed.). Ho-Ho-Kus, NJ: Thoughtful Education Press.

Stahl, R. J. (1994). *Using "think-time" and "wait-time" skillfully in the classroom.* ERIC Digest (ED370885). Bloomington, IN: ERIC Clearinghouse for Social Studies/ Social Science Education.

Strong, R. W., Hanson, J. R., & Silver, H. F. (1998). *Questioning styles & strategies* (3rd ed.). Woodbridge, NJ: Thoughtful Education Press.

Taba, H., Durkin, M. C., Fraenkel, J. R., & McNaughton, A. H. (1971). *A teachers' handbook to elementary social studies: An inductive approach* (2nd ed.). Reading, MA: Addison-Wesley.

Tanner, M., & Casados, L. (1998). Promoting and studying discussion in math classes. *Journal of Adolescent & Adult Literacy, 41*(5), 342–351.

Tredway, L. (1995). Socratic seminars: Engaging students in intellectual discourse. *Educational Leadership, 53*(1), 26–29.

Wiggins, G., & McTighe, J. (2005). *Understanding by design* (2nd ed.). Alexandria, VA: ASCD.

Wyatt, D., Pressley, M., El-Dinary, P. B., Stein, S., Evans, P., & Brown, R. (1993). Comprehension strategies, worth and credibility monitoring, and evaluations: Cold and hot cognition when experts read professional articles that are important to them. *Learning and Individual Differences, 5*, 49–72.

Zimmermann, S., & Hutchins, C. (2003). *7 keys to comprehension: How to help your kids read it and get it!* New York: Three Rivers Press.

Index

Information in figures is indicated by *f.*

About the Authors

Harvey F. Silver, EdD, is president of Silver Strong & Associates and Thoughtful Education Press. He has conducted numerous workshops for school districts and state education departments throughout the United States. He was the principal consultant for the Georgia Critical Thinking Skills Program and the Kentucky Thoughtful Education Teacher Leadership Program. With the late Richard W. Strong, he developed The Thoughtful Classroom, a renowned professional development initiative dedicated to the goal of "Making Students as Important as Standards." Dr. Silver may be reached at Silver Strong & Associates, 227 First Street, Ho-Ho-Kus, NJ 07423; 1-800-962-4432; hsilver@thoughtfulclassroom.com.

R. Thomas Dewing, EdD, has spent more than 35 years in public education as an elementary and middle school teacher, principal, instructional coordinator, and educator of gifted students. He has also taught education courses at National Louis University and North Central College. He is an experienced trainer, consultant, and presenter and has worked with numerous education organizations to create curricular teaching materials and state and national assessments. He may be reached at tdewing@thoughtful classroom.com.

Matthew J. Perini is director of publishing for Silver Strong & Associates and Thoughtful Education Press. He has authored more than 20 books, curriculum guides, articles, and research studies covering a wide range of educational topics, including learning styles, multiple intelligences, reading instruction, and effective teaching practices. He may be reached at mperini@thoughtfulclassroom.com.

Silver, Dewing, and Perini have recently collaborated on *Inference: Teaching Students to Develop Hypotheses, Evaluate Evidence, and Draw Logical Conclusions (A Strategic Teacher PLC Guide)*. With Richard W. Strong, Silver and Perini have also collaborated on a number of best sellers in education, including *The Strategic Teacher*, *So Each May Learn,* and *Teaching What Matters Most*, all published by ASCD; and Thoughtful Education Press's *Tools for Promoting Active, In-Depth Learning*, which won a Teachers' Choice Award in 2004. Most recently, Silver and Perini have developed an innovative and practical teacher evaluation model, The Thoughtful Classroom Teacher Effectiveness Framework.

Related ASCD Resources

At the time of publication, the following ASCD resources were available (ASCD stock numbers appear in parentheses). For up-to-date information about ASCD resources, go to www.ascd.org. You can search the complete archives of *Educational Leadership* at www.ascd.org/el.

Go to www.ascd.org/commoncore to find a variety of ASCD resources on Common Core State Standards, including Professional Development Institutes, webinars, PD In Focus, PD Online courses, DVDs, and books.

Online Course
Visit www.ascd.org for the following professional development opportunity:
- *The Core Six: Teaching with the Common Core in Mind* by Harvey F. Silver, R. Thomas Dewing, and Matthew J. Perini (#PD12OC004).

Print Products
- *Common Core Standards for High School English Language Arts: A Quick-Start Guide* by Susan Ryan and Dana Frazee (#113010)
- *Compare & Contrast: Teaching Comparative Thinking to Strengthen Student Learning (A Strategic Teacher PLC Guide)* by Harvey F. Silver (#110126)
- *Inference: Teaching Students to Develop Hypotheses, Evaluate Evidence, and Draw Logical Conclusions (A Strategic Teacher PLC Guide)* by Harvey F. Silver, R. Thomas Dewing, and Matthew J. Perini (#112027)
- *The Interactive Lecture: How to Engage Students, Build Memory, and Deepen Comprehension (A Strategic Teacher PLC Guide)* by Harvey F. Silver and Matthew J. Perini (#110127)
- *Reading for Meaning: How to Build Students' Comprehension, Reasoning, and Problem-Solving Skills (A Strategic Teacher PLC Guide)* by Harvey F. Silver, Susan C. Morris, and Victor Klein (#110128)
- *The Strategic Teacher: Selecting the Right Research-Based Strategy for Every Lesson* by Harvey F. Silver, Richard W. Strong, and Matthew J. Perini (#107059)
- *Task Rotation: Strategies for Differentiating Activities and Assessments by Learning Style (A Strategic Teacher PLC Guide)* by Harvey F. Silver, Joyce W. Jackson, and Daniel R. Moirao (#110129)
- *Teaching What Matters Most: Standards and Strategies for Raising Student Achievement* by Harvey F. Silver, Matthew J. Perini, and Richard W. Strong (#100057)
- *Understanding Common Core State Standards* by John Kendall (#112011)

Video and DVD
- The Strategic Teacher (DVD) (#610137)

THE WHOLE CHILD The Whole Child Initiative helps schools and communities create learning environments that allow students to be healthy, safe, engaged, supported, and challenged. To learn more about other books and resources that relate to the whole child, visit www.wholechildeducation.org.

For more information: send e-mail to member@ascd.org; call 1-800-933-2723 or 703-578-9600, press 2; send a fax to 703-575-5400; or write to Information Services, ASCD, 1703 N. Beauregard St., Alexandria, VA 22311-1714 USA.